Escape from Saigon

By the same author

Orphan Train Rider: One Boy's True Story
Pioneer Girl: Growing Up on the Prairie
Surviving Hitler: A Boy in the Nazi Death Camps
We Rode the Orphan Trains

Escape from Saigon

How a Vietnam War Orphan Became an American Boy

Andrea Warren

SQUARE FISH

Farrar Straus Giroux

SQUARE
FISH

An Imprint of Macmillan

Library of Congress Cataloging-in-Publication Data
Warren, Andrea.
    Escape from Saigon : how a Vietnam War orphan became an American boy / Andrea Warren.
        p.   cm.
    Summary: Chronicles the experiences of an orphaned Amerasian boy from his birth and early childhood
in Saigon through his departure from Vietnam in the 1975 Operation Babylift and his subsequent life
as the adopted son of an American family in Ohio, and his return to Vietnam.
    ISBN 978-0-374-40023-1
    1. Steiner, Matt—Juvenile literature. 2. Vietnamese Americans—Biography—Juvenile literature
3. Adopted children—United States—Biography—Juvenile literature. 4. Orphans—Vietnam—
Biography—Juvenile literature. 5. Vietnamese Conflict, 1961–1975—Children—Juvenile literature.
6. Vietnamese Conflict, 1961–1975—Refugees—Juvenile literature. 7. Ho Chi Minh City (Vietnam)—
Biography—Juvenile literature. [1. Steiner, Matt. 2. Vietnamese Americans—Biography. 3. Vietnamese
Conflict, 1961–1975—Children. 4. Intercountry adoption. 5. Interracial adoption. 6. Adoption.] I. Title.
    E184.V53S74 2004   959.704'3'086*45—dc22   2003060672

Originally published in the United States by Farrar Straus Giroux
First Square Fish Edition: February 2012
Square Fish logo designed by Filomena Tuosto
mackids.com

10 9 8 7 6 5

AR: 6.2 / LEXILE: 930L

For Alison,
born in my heart

The author's Vietnamese daughter, Alison (center, baseball cap),
with children in the Mekong Delta region of Vietnam,
near the orphanage where she once lived

War, no end to it, people scattered in all directions . . .
—PHUNG KHAC KHOAN
Vietnamese poet, 1528–1613

Contents

A Note to Readers

The events I recount in this book are based on documented historical fact and the recollections of those whose stories appear, and as memories are necessarily subjective, they may differ from those of others. I have reconstructed conversations from the memories of these individuals, bearing in mind that many of the incidents in this story occurred in the 1970s and that people rarely have perfect recall after so many years.

Introduction

I will never forget the fear. In the first days of April 1975, the baby daughter we had never seen was trapped in Saigon, South Vietnam, half a world away from us. Alice Spring was only six months old. She had been brought to Saigon for medical treatment from her orphanage deep in the Mekong Delta. When her health improved, Friends For All Children, the humanitarian agency we had worked with for two years in hopes of adopting a Vietnamese orphan, told us about her. Would we be interested?

Yes! we cried. Send her immediately! That was in January 1975. We knew it would take until summer to complete paperwork so she could come to us. We settled in to wait, loving her from afar.

But in March it suddenly became clear that South Vietnam was about to fall to the North Vietnamese forces. We began to wonder if we would ever hold our baby girl. In a very short time, Saigon was surrounded by Communist troops. The only safe way out of the city was by air, and commercial airliners were no longer flying into Saigon.

It seemed like a miracle when the American government responded to pleas for help to evacuate the orphans in Saigon who were already assigned to adoptive homes abroad. Our hearts were filled with joy.

But on April 4, we awoke to the horrifying news that the first planeload of orphans on Operation Babylift had crashed. The children were from our agency, Friends For All Children, and many were dead. Was Alice Spring on that flight? When we finally learned she was not, we rejoiced, even as we grieved for the families who had lost their children.

Today, Alice Spring, renamed Alison, is a happy, healthy adult—a college graduate and a mother. Growing up, she remembered nothing about being evacuated in the nick of time from a doomed city, nor did she remember her homeland. In 1996, shortly after Vietnam reopened to the West, our family journeyed with Alison to see that homeland. We were enchanted by the beauty of the country, the warmth of the people, and the delicious cuisine—all part of the rich Vietnamese culture.

But the highlight of our journey was meeting the brave and wonderful people, many of them Catholic nuns, who had cared for Alison as an infant and made certain, when she became sick, that she got to Saigon and to help. We saw Newhaven, the care center sponsored by Friends For All Children, where she grew strong during the months leading up to the Babylift. With us on the trip was Mary Nelle Gage, a Sister of Loretto from Colorado who had worked at Newhaven. We also met with Rosemary Taylor, the Australian at the heart of Friends For All Children, who many believe single-handedly did more to assist the orphanages and orphaned children of South Vietnam than any other person during the war. She explained the challenges of trying to care for overwhelming numbers of children, many very ill, in a country at war, with too few supplies and too little medicine.

We returned from our trip humbled by the devotion of these volunteers in South Vietnam, both the Vietnamese and those from other countries. My daughter owes her life to them, and so do thousands of other adoptees and other Vietnamese children.

I have long felt that the story of the plight of the war orphans, and of the Babylift itself, needed to be told. With my daughter unable to remember what happened to her at so young an age, I looked for an older Babylift child with memories of that fateful time. Matt Steiner, who was eight years old when he was evacuated, turned out to be that person. Unlike my daughter, who is full-blooded Vietnamese, Matt is Amerasian, with a Vietnamese mother and an unknown American father. When his family could no longer provide for him, he was fortunate, just as Alison was, to be cared for by an international relief agency that could help him find an adoptive family. Matt and Alison both know they were lucky, even if Alison never knew her biological parents and Matt lost his.

Innocent children have always been the victims of war, and never more so than in the last century. At the beginning of the twentieth century, 90 percent of war casualties were soldiers. In the last decade of that century, 90 percent of the casualties were civilians. Many of those were children. More than 1.5 million children died in the Holocaust of World War II. In the 1990s, more than two million children died in wars around the globe.

Orphaned children, and those left behind by parents unable to care for them, are also the victims of war. In South Vietnam, more than a million

A young boy and his brother flee the fighting in South Vietnam's central highlands

children were orphaned by the war and only a few thousand made it to adoptive families. Of the rest, some found their way to relatives, if they were fortunate enough to have them. Others tried to live on the streets, fending for themselves, while still others were taken to orphanages, where they might grow up if they were lucky enough to get the food they needed and if they didn't catch a fatal disease. Some never grew up at all, but instead turned their faces to the wall and refused nourishment, perhaps because even at such a tender age, they'd had enough of the world.

As you read this story of the other side of war—not of soldiers and battles, but of orphans and people trying to help them—my hope is that you will think of all the other children in this world whose lives are scarred by war. And when you have the opportunity, I hope that you will do whatever you can to help children, wherever they live, who are in harm's way and cannot help themselves.

Prologue

Vietnam is an ancient land, both beautiful and mysterious. It lies along the eastern coast of Southeast Asia, half a world away from the United States. It is rich in natural resources, and since its earliest history, these riches have been coveted by other nations.

Though Vietnam has been conquered many times, its people have always fought valiantly to expel invaders, including the Chinese, who ruled Vietnam for a thousand years, ending in the early part of the tenth century. The French arrived in Vietnam in 1859 and left in defeat in 1954.

That same year, because of conflict over who would control the country, Vietnam split in two. North Vietnam was under Communist rule, and South Vietnam struggled to establish an independent republic. Both North and South wanted a unified nation, but each wanted its own form of government. Thus began the long war between the two Vietnams, a war that would take many lives and leave no family untouched by sorrow.

*Divided into North and South in 1954, Vietnam hugs the coast of Southeast
Asia along the South China Sea*

Escape from Saigon

A LITTLE BOY ALL ALONE

His mother gave him the simple Vietnamese name of Long.

When he was born in 1966, Long's mother—whose name he no longer recalls—was living with his American father. Deep in memory, Long carries a vague image of this man. It's like a photo. In it, he sees his parents together. His father has blue eyes and hair the color of sand. He towers over Long's petite Vietnamese mother, so lovely, with silky black hair and laughing brown eyes. They look very happy.

Long doesn't think they were married, nor does he know why his father had come to Southeast Asia during the Vietnam War. He might have been a soldier or a businessman. All Long knows is that by the time he was two, his father was gone. And his mother was never happy again.

Long does not know why his mother wanted to live in Saigon. Because of the war, she might have thought they were safe there, since it was the capital of South Vietnam and an important base for the military. Known as the Paris of the Orient, the city captivated the senses with its tropical flowers, graceful palm trees, constant crush of people and traffic, its bright sun and unrelenting heat. In the midst of war, it was full of energy, intrigue, and excitement.

Many Americans were in Saigon. The United States supported South Vietnam's struggle against the Communists of North Vietnam. With the assistance of other democratic nations, in 1961 the U.S. began to send ad-

*Saigon in the 1950s, when it was known as the Paris of the Orient. Bicycles
and cyclos were, and still are, a popular form of transportation*

visers and then troops to help in the conflict. By 1965, nearly two hundred
thousand American soldiers were serving in the Vietnam War, fighting
alongside the South Vietnamese.

The American government had its embassy and military headquarters
in Saigon. In 1968, shortly before Long and his mother arrived in the city,
the Communists launched an all-out assault on South Vietnam. They almost took over the American embassy, and there was fighting in the streets
of Saigon. Because of this, security was tight in the city, and soldiers were
everywhere. Long soon got used to seeing military jeeps, trucks, and soldiers on the streets. He learned that if you begged for candy and gum from
the friendly American GIs, you usually got it.

When Long was three or four, he and his mother moved in with a Viet-

During the decade Americans fought in South Vietnam, children in villages as well as cities discovered that many GIs were friendly, and often carried candy and gum for them

namese man. It's possible his mother married this man, for Long thought of him as his stepfather. The man had a son, an older boy Long called his step-brother. The four of them lived in a tiny apartment in a rundown neigh-borhood near the Saigon River. They had no electricity or indoor plumbing. When they needed to go to the bathroom, they waited their turn at the wooden stalls lined up along the banks of the river.

The war had little reality for Long. What was real was how his violent stepfather treated his mother. When he struck her, Long tried to protect her.

In 1971, when he was five, Long and his mother fled the city to escape his stepfather. In the village where Long's mother had grown up, they crowded in with relatives. There was always someone just a few steps away. One of them was Long's grandmother, called Ba. He liked Ba, who was tiny

Today, homes in rural Vietnamese villages look much like they always have.
Long may have lived in a house like this one

Caught in a crossfire, two village children cling to their mothers as an
American paratrooper searches for Vietcong snipers

and feisty and cooked delicious, spicy food. Ba often chewed a seed called betel nut, which had turned her teeth dark. Many Vietnamese, especially older ones, chewed betel nut, believing it improved their health and protected their teeth from decay.

The village, which sat at the edge of a jungle, was its own separate world. While the adults and older children worked in the rice paddies outside the village, the old folks like Ba cared for the young children.

During the year that Long and his mother lived there, war did not disturb the village. But in many other areas, villagers lived in constant fear of soldiers. They also feared the South Vietnamese who were Vietcong (short for Vietnamese Communists), guerrilla fighters who sided with the North. The Vietcong did not wear military uniforms. Instead, they looked the same as the South Vietnamese villagers, making it very difficult to detect them. At any time, the Vietcong might raid a village, taking all the villagers' food, killing their livestock and burning their homes, and even torturing or killing the villagers themselves.

Trouble could also come from soldiers of the South Vietnamese army, who were looking for Vietcong or their sympathizers. During the decade that American soldiers fought in the war, they, too, might terrorize a village in their search for "Charlie"—their name for the Vietcong. Whole villages could be destroyed by any of these soldiers, or villages might be bombed from the air. Some villagers were killed while working in their rice paddies or while trying to protect their families.

But in Long's village, these terrible things had never happened. And in spite of food shortages affecting the entire country, he had enough to eat.

Long adapted easily to village life. He was always barefoot and wore shorts and cotton shirts. Though his mother had worn dresses in the city, here she wore pants and long-sleeved shirts to work in the humid heat of the rice paddies. When she pinned her hair under the cone-shaped cane hat she wore to keep the hot sun off her face, she looked like any other villager.

A special treat for Long was riding the big water buffaloes used to help with the work. These animals were the villagers' tractors. Long looked forward to the day he could be a real buffalo boy and help take care of the great beasts. Sometimes his mother took him out to the rice paddies so he could see how the rice was growing. He liked walking along the dikes, but kept a careful watch for snakes and lizards.

Long wanted to become a buffalo boy like the boy shown here

Though the villagers worked hard, they also had good times. Storytelling was considered an art, and storytellers drew appreciative audiences who listened intently to their retellings of old legends and folktales. Some villagers enjoyed chess and card games. Others played musical instruments while villagers sang and danced. Every holiday was a village celebration.

Each morning, Long attended classes in the one-room schoolhouse, where he sat on a wooden bench with the other children. He wished he could go to school all day, but only children whose parents could afford to pay extra tuition were allowed to do that. In the afternoons, after he had helped Ba sweep the house, gather firewood, or weed the small family garden, he had the run of the village.

Long was an easygoing little boy with a big smile, and he readily made friends. If any of the villagers were disturbed by the fact that he was half white, he does not remember it. "When I was very young, I looked like the other children," he says. "I had black hair, brown eyes, and my skin was dark enough that I could blend in. As I grew older, it became more obvious that I was half white. What set me apart from the other children when I was young wasn't the way I looked, but that I had no father. I didn't mind. My mother was gentle and sweet. I didn't feel the loss of a father, as long as I had her."

But something wasn't right with his mother. She slept more and more, ate little, and grew silent. She lost interest in village life. She still took excellent care of Long, but she seemed distant. Only rarely could Long get her to smile.

One day she took him on a walk across the fields and rice paddies and along a jungle path. They reached a road where an automobile was waiting. Long had never been in a car, and found it a great curiosity. It was large and shiny. The door opened, and Long's mother urged him to get in. He climbed into the backseat, expecting her to join him. Before he knew what was happening, the car sped away. His mother still stood by the road.

Long panicked. He cried her name, but the car would not stop. When at last it did, the driver had brought Long to a vast plantation that had once belonged to the French. There, a Vietnamese couple tried to make him feel welcome. They offered him toys, food, and new clothes. They were very kind to him. They said they owned the plantation, which would be his new home, and they would be his new parents.

But he would have none of it. Where was his mother? He wanted his mother! Whenever anyone tried to talk to him or come near him, he shrieked at the top of his lungs. All day and all night, for several days and nights, he cried and carried on. He refused to eat, even though his stomach rumbled from hunger.

Finally, the couple gave up. Long was put in the car and returned to the place where his mother had left him. She met him there, her face without expression, and took him back to the village. Long was bewildered. Why had his mother tried to give him away? She would not answer him, and in his relief to be back with her, he did not ask again.

A few months later, in 1972, when Long was six, the world as he knew it ended. Awakening one morning on the sleeping mat next to his mother's, he was surprised that she was not yet up. He shook her, then realized how still she was.

He screamed, and his grandmother rushed in. "What is it?" Ba cried. Trembling, Long pointed at the silent form on the mat. Ba touched her daughter's cold face. When she could not awaken her, she began to wail. Other family members quickly gathered around. Long's beautiful mother was dead.

How had such a terrible thing happened? No one knew for sure, but later Long heard relatives say that she had probably taken poison.

"I have only fragments of memory of what happened after that," Long says. "For several days, relatives crowded the house. They prepared my mother's body for a Buddhist burial in the village cemetery. They wrapped her in white cloth and put a ball of sweet rice in her mouth. It had coins pressed into it. This was to give her food and money for her journey into the spirit world. There was a funeral procession through the village, and I remember the smell of sandalwood and incense. Everyone was chanting and crying. I didn't understand what was happening."

Adding to the horror of losing his mother were the whispered concerns of relatives who feared for her soul because she had taken her own life. They spoke of the judgment she was now enduring in the afterlife, and the difficult journey she must make out of darkness. They worried that because she died in a negative state of mind, her unhappiness would travel with her when she was reborn into a new life, and cause her misfortune.

Long was frightened for his mother. Was she suffering? Ba and his aunts and uncles tried to comfort him, but his heart was filled with misery. He had never felt so alone.

"My mother had been my whole world. Once she had tried to give me away. Now she had abandoned me forever. How could she do this to me? Did she really love me?"

Another worry loomed larger than anything else. Without his mother to care for him, he wondered over and over, "What will happen to me?"

A NEW LIFE IN SAIGON

Soon after his mother's death, Ba told Long she was taking him back to Saigon to live. "I don't know why we left our family in the village," he says. "Life was difficult for us in the city."

They moved into a one-room apartment that opened onto an alley. Though Ba was elderly, she worked long hours at several jobs to support her six-year-old grandson and herself.

It was still hard to afford food. Just a year and a half earlier, when Long had lived in Saigon with his mother, the city was full of opportunity. But the United States had not been able to win the Vietnam War. After nearly a decade of trying, the government had yielded to pressure from the American people to bring their soldiers home. They were leaving the South Vietnamese to try to win the war without American troop support. When Ba and Long arrived in 1972, the withdrawal was under way. Many businesses in Saigon had catered to the Americans. As the soldiers gradually left, unemployment increased and inflation slowly drove up prices.

Ba stretched every penny. She was an excellent cook. Long thought she could make anything taste good, and she always made the hot, spicy stir-fry dishes and noodle bowls he loved. But too soon his stomach begged for more than the small helpings she was able to give him.

While Ba worked, Long was on his own. In the mornings, he attended classes at the neighborhood primary school. He was a good student and discovered a special interest in math. When school ended at noon, he hung around the streets with neighborhood boys. They played games like hide-and-seek, tag, and war. They spun tops and played marbles. They went to the river and watched the fishing boats, barges, and ferries. Sometimes on their way to a park where they liked to play, they passed by a movie theater and stopped to look at the posters, wishing aloud that they had a few coins so they could go inside.

More than anything else, Long dreamed of having a bicycle. Then he could go where he wanted, and go quickly. Maybe he would be a cyclo (*see-klo*) driver when he grew up. He would pedal his bike around Saigon all day, looking for customers who would sit on the low seat attached to the front of the bike and pay him to take them where they needed to go.

The streets he liked best were the ones built by the French during the hundred years they had occupied Vietnam. Tall, arching trees banked the wide boulevards, and wrought-iron gates and balconies decorated the pastel-colored buildings. Long admired the Catholic cathedral that dominated one intersection, and wondered what it was like inside.

But he was rarely in that part of the city. He and Ba lived in a very poor area. At least they had an apartment. Some poor people lived on the Saigon River in tiny boats called sampans or in makeshift shanties that clung to the river's banks. Whenever fighting became fierce in the countryside, refugees poured into the city, looking for shelter and food. Many had to crowd into rickety slum apartments already stuffed with people.

Long often saw homeless children living on the streets, struggling to find enough to eat and sleeping anywhere they could. He knew they were orphans, and he felt sorry for them. Because he had his grandmother, it did not occur to Long that he too was an orphan or that, like many of the street children, he was a mixed-blood child—an Amerasian, with an Asian mother and an American father. Nor did it occur to him that these children were

With space in short supply, many Vietnamese in the 1960s lived in crowded conditions on sampans or in tiny shacks perched on stilts over the river. This is true even today

even more hungry than he was, even though he sometimes saw them trying to find small scraps of food in garbage cans—something he had never had to do.

But like these children, food was his main interest. He always stopped to watch people order food from the many street vendors whose tiny food stands lined the sidewalks. How he wished he had money to do that. One specialty people ordered was *pho*, a flavorful noodle soup eaten for breakfast and throughout the day. Many people liked their soup served with spring rolls: thin, soft sheets of rice paper wrapped around fillings of fine noodles and slivers of vegetables. Sometimes they were steamed, and sometimes fried crispy. Either way, they were dipped in tiny cups of *nuoc mam*, a spicy fermented fish sauce.

Another street delicacy was squares of custard tied up in strong green leaves so they looked like exquisite little packages. Some vendors sold French bread and soft drinks. Long's favorite street food was a meat sandwich made with fresh French bread. Ba bought this sandwich for him one time as a special treat. Long thought it was one of the best things he had ever eaten. He watched enviously, his mouth watering, whenever he saw someone buying one.

Eating at an outdoor stall is still a daily treat for many Vietnamese

His favorite place to visit was the large open-air market near his neighborhood. Few people had refrigerators or freezers, so they bought fresh food every day at the street markets. There were always dozens of kinds of fresh fish, and even live eels, snakes, turtles, and pigeons—all considered delicacies. "Dee-licious!" the vendors called out to shoppers.

Long usually stopped to watch the caged pigs and the ducks, geese, and chickens tied together in bundles. He wondered if they knew they were destined to be someone's dinner. Once the animals were purchased, some customers took them home alive. Others made a selection, and the vendor butchered the luckless creature on the spot. This was accompanied by an explosion of squawking or squealing, followed by the pungent odor of blood. Long was repulsed and fascinated all at once.

He enjoyed watching customers haggle over purchases. He knew from shopping with Ba that no one ever expected to pay the asking price, and he waited with anticipation when the bargaining started. People always stopped to watch, and some even participated in the often heated negotiations. Once both sides agreed on a price, everyone was full of smiles.

Nothing tantalized Long's senses as much as the market. He loved all the colors, smells, and textures. He inhaled the scents of all the different spices and herbs, like lemon grass, ginger, cilantro, coriander, cinnamon, and mint. He liked the interesting textures of the mounds of rice and coffee beans, and all the varieties of handmade noodles. There were many types of chilies, tofu, and vegetables. The fruits, with their varied colors, shapes, and textures, were his favorite. He could name them all: longans, jackfruit, coconuts, kumquats, melons, papayas, pineapples, mangos, lychees, persimmons, rambutans, and many types of bananas.

But the market always increased his hunger. When his friends were with him, sooner or later one of them snatched something, usually a piece of fruit. When that happened, someone would yell, "Run!" and they would all take off, shrieking with laughter. Later they shared the stolen gem, rarely getting more than a small bite each.

"The fun part was being chased by an angry vendor," Long says. "We never got caught."

Sudden rainstorms were a daily event, even when it wasn't the rainy season. They began with no warning, dropping sheets of rain that sent everyone scurrying for shelter. Vendors quickly covered their stands in plastic. Cyclo drivers hastily draped coverings over passengers, and anyone with an umbrella pulled it out. Long and his friends either huddled under a store awning or played in the warm rain. It would stop as suddenly as it had started, and the boys would go about their business.

All the moisture kept flowers blooming and grass a lush green. But the high humidity slowed everyone down, and sometimes in the heat of the afternoon, the boys looked for hidden places in the bustling city where they could take naps.

When his grandmother came home, always exhausted from her day, Long greeted her, and they settled into their evening together. Long helped her prepare dinner and then clean up. As their room grew shadowy, Ba lit the large oil lamp and Long did his schoolwork. He enjoyed talking to Ba about her day or about things he had seen on the street. Although he missed his mother very much, he grew increasingly attached to his grandmother.

When it was Tet, the three-day New Year's celebration that occurred in late January or early February, Ba made sure Long had a new outfit of colorful silk. Ba wore her *ao dai (ow zai)*, the traditional high-necked, long-sleeved tunic, slit to the waist on both sides, and worn over full silk slacks. The two of them said extra prayers at the temple and also at the small altar in their apartment, for at Tet, the belief is that the ancestors come home to visit, and Ba wanted to make them welcome.

In the city, Tet was far more elaborate than it had been in the village. "Tet was like Thanksgiving, Christmas, and the Fourth of July, all rolled into one," Long says. "We had celebrations and parades, sparklers, fireworks to ward off evil spirits, ringing bells, and special foods. My very favorite event was the elaborate dragon parade. We all wore costumes for that. On the actual New Year's day, everyone—no matter when they were born during the year—celebrated his or her birthday and officially turned another year older."

Whenever she could, Ba took Long to the neighborhood temple. "I liked to see the large statue of the Buddha and hear the chanting of the monks," he says. "My grandmother taught me the Buddhist beliefs—that you strive always to be good, that you show compassion toward others, and that you practice patience in all things."

Long realized that patience might ease, but did not eliminate, their struggles. "I knew Ba was concerned about our situation. We were trying to stretch our rice further and further. But even though we sometimes went hungry, we took food offerings to the temple, where we lit incense and prayed for my mother. I did not have a clear understanding of where her soul was or whether she was struggling, but I hoped I was helping her by leaving the food. I was angry at her for leaving me and very sad that she was dead.

"I would have done anything to bring her back. I could feel a hole in my heart in the place where she should be."

~

For more than a year, Ba and Long lived in the tiny apartment and managed to get by. But times grew harder.

"I could see the worry in my grandmother's eyes," Long says. "With the American soldiers gone, many in South Vietnam feared a takeover by North Vietnam. No one knew just what that would mean for us. The city seemed safe, but who really knew? We saw jeeps and military trucks and soldiers all the time. We had to be off the streets by eleven at night because we had an enforced curfew. Most nights, we heard shelling outside the city."

Though Long took care of himself during the day, his grandmother saw that he needed more supervision, that he was spending too much time on the streets with nothing to do. She worried that as he got older, he would start to get into trouble.

"She spent what time she could with me. She wished she could send me to school all day, because I was an eager student and school would keep me occupied, but she did not have an extra penny for that. Mostly, she worried that the day would come when she could no longer feed me."

On Long's seventh birthday, May 15, 1973, Ba said they had an appointment and that it was a long distance away. She would say no more. They set out on foot through the streets. They had walked a long time when Ba stopped at a street vendor's stall. To the boy's delight, she bought him his favorite meat sandwich—his birthday present.

As he ate, she began to tell him that something very special was about to happen. She had learned of a place that would take him in. It was a good place, she said.

Her voice broke, but she continued. These people, who were Americans, would find him a new family. This would be the best thing for him. It might even be a family in America. It would be better for him there, she said. He could go to school and would have enough to eat. And he would have a new mother.

"You would like to have a mother again, wouldn't you?" she asked.

He hesitated. Could there be such a thing as a *new* mother? He took his grandmother's hand. "I have you, Ba."

"I can no longer take care of you," she said softly.

Long tried to understand her words. Then he realized her meaning. She *couldn't* take care of him. He felt a rush of fear. Somehow he had learned to live without his mother. But what would he do if Ba left him?

Finally they arrived at a plain three-story building with the address Ba was looking for. The sign said it was the Holt Center. Long could hear children playing. What was this place? Inside the building he waited on a hallway bench while Ba sat in an office and talked to a Vietnamese woman and an American man. Long saw his grandmother sign some papers. When she came out, she had tears in her eyes. She hugged him goodbye and promised to visit when she could.

The Holt Center in Saigon

"I know you will be a good boy," she said. "Do whatever they tell you to do."

As the door closed behind her, Long tried not to panic. When would he see her again? How could she leave him, when his mother had done the same thing? He wanted to run after her, hold on tight, and never let go.

He stayed on the bench, staring at the closed door. For the first time in his life, he was on his own. He took a deep breath, struggling to swallow the lump in his throat. He did not understand what was going on, but until his grandmother returned for him, he would try to be brave.

AT HOME AT HOLT

At recess, Long kept an eye on the bicycles. He watched the riders carefully. How did you balance yourself on two slim wheels? Could he teach himself to do that? He had no chance to try, as other children were always on the few bikes. He dreamed of being the rider, circling around the playground, going faster than anyone could run.

Seven-year-old Long, shortly after his arrival at the Holt Center, holding a card with his name and birthdate

The children tried to get him to join their games, but he stayed apart, waiting. Ba would come back for him. He was sure of this. Whenever he was near the front gate, he looked out anxiously, watching for her.

While he waited, he tried not to call attention to himself. He slept in the bunk he was assigned to, ate the food placed in front of him, and sat obediently in his classes. Of the hundred children at the Holt Center,

Like children everywhere, the kids at Holt could turn any object into a plaything

twenty-five were near his age. Almost all of them were Amerasian, many of them half black. Long quickly figured out which children were best friends, who was the most skilled at jumping rope, and who told funny jokes. The best bike rider was Ky, who was half black and taller than Long. He was friendly and outgoing and well liked by the other children.

Most of the staff were Vietnamese, but there were also several Americans. Long saw little resemblance between himself and the Americans. They seemed tall and pale, at least compared to the smaller, darker-skinned, brown-eyed, black-haired Vietnamese staff. Americans had round eyes that might be green or blue, and hair colors that were just as strange—blond, brown, and even red. Instead of the simple clothing worn by Vietnamese, their clothing had more pockets, belts, buttons, and collars. The men wore shoes and socks instead of rubber sandals. Still, Long liked them. Americans smiled a lot, and they were nice to the children.

But Long's favorite adults were the Vietnamese teachers. He liked his teacher best. The children called her Miss Anh. She was pretty and patient and lots of fun, and Long felt comfortable around her.

Even his first day at Holt, Long heard the word "adoption." It was Ky who explained to him what it was. A week after Long's arrival, he was sitting by himself under a tree on the playground, watching the other children. Ky rode over on a bike, laid it on its side, and plopped down beside him.

"See that girl with braids?" he said, pointing. "Her name is Amy. It's an American name. Her new family gave it to her and she's already started using it. She's leaving soon to go to them in California."

"California?" Long did not understand.

"It's a place in America. She's being adopted. That means getting a new family. When someone says they'll adopt you, everyone signs a paper. Then you get on an airplane and fly clear across the ocean to live with your new family."

Was this what his grandmother had meant when she spoke of a new family for him? Long wondered.

"Does 'adopted' mean a new mother?" he asked.

Ky nodded. "And a house and everything."

Long grew thoughtful. Adoption. Was this something he would like? He didn't want to go far from Ba. But he would like a home, and especially a mother. "What is it like in America?" he finally asked.

"They have horses and a million cars and oceans and lakes and mountains," Ky said. "It's so big, you can't drive across it in a day." He stood up, pointing at the bike. "Want to try? It's not too hard."

Long (on the right) and several friends pause for a moment during their play

Long eyed the bike. He really did want to.

"I'll hold it for you, so you won't fall over."

With a shy grin, Long got to his feet. The other kids immediately came to help out, and soon Long was riding around the playground, thrilled with his new skill. By the end of the day, he was part of the group, and within another day or two, he was one of its leaders.

~

Though Long did not yet understand it, Ba had placed him in the care of Holt International Children's Services, headquartered in Eugene, Oregon. Holt was well known for helping orphaned children born in other countries find adoptive homes in America.

Somehow Long's grandmother had heard about Holt. One day she left her work and went to the Center without Long and talked to a Vietnamese social worker. She worried that it was difficult for her to make enough money to feed her grandson. But she also worried that she was old, and if something happened to her, Long would not have family to protect him from discrimination he might suffer because he was Amerasian. Could Holt help?

The social worker had assured Ba that the Holt agency would try to find a family for Long. It might take a while, and there was little possibility it would be with a Vietnamese family. Instead, it would probably be in America. Ba wept when she agreed to this, knowing it meant she would never see her grandson again.

The social workers at Holt often heard stories like Ba's. Holt wanted to help Vietnamese children who either had no family or whose families could not care for them. Other child assistance groups working in South Vietnam also wanted to help. The need was overwhelming. The upheaval of the war had created a country of refugees, with people constantly moving around, trying to stay out of harm's way. Many of the refugees had come from North Vietnam, leaving their homeland because they did not want to live under Communism.

The Vietnamese have always believed that as long as you have relatives, you have a home. But the many years of war had so weakened the family structure that this was not always true. Mothers died from illness. Fathers were away in the army or had been killed. Sometimes families were separated while fleeing enemy troops. If parents could no longer feed their children, they might take them to orphanages, perhaps planning to return for them later, if they could. Or they might leave them in public places, hoping they would be found and cared for. Only 25,000 of South Vietnam's estimated one million orphans lived in the country's approximately one hundred orphanages. The rest lived with one relative or another, or fended for themselves.

In 1973, Holt opened its first center in Saigon to assist families in cri-

Many orphans, like this young boy and his baby sister, begged on the streets of Saigon to support themselves

sis. Sometimes they cared for severely malnourished babies and children, working very hard to save these children's lives and return them to good health. While in Holt's care, the children lived at the Holt Center. The staff tried to find adoptive homes for children who were orphaned or whose parents could no longer care for them. Sadly, because of the hardships of the war, few Vietnamese could adopt a child. Most of the children went to live with American families. Babies waiting to be adopted did not stay at the Holt Center. Instead, children two and under lived with Vietnamese foster families until it was time for them to leave for their new homes.

The older the child, the harder it was to find an adoptive home. For older Amerasian children like Long, it was hardest of all.

~

After a month at Holt, Long was still getting used to new ways of doing things. The first time he pushed the handle on a flush toilet, he jumped back, startled by the swirling water. It seemed peculiar to be going to the bathroom inside a house instead of outside. Taking a shower was also odd. Long was used to washing with some water and a rag. A shower was like standing in warm rain, only you used soap and shampoo.

But the strangest thing was learning to eat with a fork. Long had never used anything except chopsticks. It was easy to pick up food with those. Trying to stab something with four prongs made little sense to him.

The food was also different. Long wasn't used to much meat or to sweets. The cook at Holt used lots of rice and noodles, foods he loved, but added things like canned beef. Whoever thought that meat could come in a can! The cook made pudding, which he liked, and cookies and cakes. Nobody seemed to mind how much he ate, and his thin frame began to fill out.

Good food and plenty of it was one of the best things about Holt. Long

Mealtime at Holt is full of activity

also liked being with the other children, especially the boys his age. One day Ky decided to teach him to tie shoelaces. Long didn't have any shoes, nor did the other children, except for the rubber sandals they sometimes wore, but Ky said that in America, children wore shoes, and you needed to know how to tie the laces. He learned with a pair of laces belonging to Miss Anh, their teacher, struggling to master the art of looping and threading, until he could produce a strong knot with both laces the same length. He couldn't imagine he would ever need to know this strange American skill.

Because all the children were waiting for new families, they talked constantly about adoption. On a bulletin board near the administrative offices on the first floor was a large map of the United States with colored pins stuck in states where children had already gone. Amy proudly pointed to California and pulled out the photo of her new family, which she always kept with her.

"You want to see it?"

Long did. His eyes went past Amy's new sisters and father to the blond woman with the big smile. Amy said her new mother had written a letter saying how much she was looking forward to meeting her new daughter. She said Amy would have her own bedroom.

Long was surprised. "Why would you want that? It's better to sleep near people."

"Not there," Amy said uncertainly. "Americans are rich. They have their own rooms."

"Won't you be scared?"

Amy said she hoped it wouldn't be too bad, though she agreed it was better to sleep close to other people. She also said she should be leaving for America in the late fall. "I'll be there for Christmas," she informed him.

"What's that?"

She looked unsure. "I think it's like Tet. Only you don't wear costumes. And you cut a tree, and put it in your house and decorate it."

Long laughed. Americans did some strange things. But from what he had heard, America was still a good place. Americans had plenty of food, and they were far from war. They had lots of schools and colleges, and when you grew up, you could be anything you wanted. It was hard to believe that was true—didn't your family decide that for you?

Long studied the hallway map, trying to learn the names of the states and wondering what each one was like. But when he thought about America, he worried about Ba. How could he leave his grandmother behind? Shouldn't he stay at the Holt Center so he could see her once in a while? So far she had not come to visit. He missed her very much, and if he went to America, he could *never* see her.

His days settled into a routine of school and play. School was held on the flat roof of the building. It was hot up there, especially during the summer, but at least there were tentlike coverings to provide shade. Long liked peering between the railings at people on the sidewalk below. He liked looking at the buildings around them, and seeing planes take off and land at nearby Tan Son Nhut Airport. Someday maybe he would be on one of those airplanes, flying off to meet his new family.

On Holt's rooftop school, teachers help students with their schoolwork and craft projects

It seemed like every week or two, several children left to go to new homes. Usually it was younger children, but whenever it was one of the older ones, he felt anxious. What if no one ever wanted him? Or what if someone *did* want him and he had to leave? He didn't like thinking about going so far from Ba and from the place where he had his memories of his mother.

He couldn't complain about being at Holt. He felt safe and well cared for. There was usually something fun to do. Sometimes the children went on special outings. They walked to a nearby pool to swim, or they played at parks in the area. One time they went to the Saigon zoo. There were only a few animals left because the zoo did not have money to care for more. Those that remained looked thin and sad. The tiger had lost clumps of hair. Miss Anh said it was because the tiger didn't have enough to eat. Once the zoo had been the pride of the city. Maybe, if the war ever ended, it could be again.

Miss Anh became Long's special friend. She reminded him of his mother because of the gentle way she treated him and because of her soft laugh. Several times she took him to visit her home and eat with her family. She lived with her parents and two brothers, and they always welcomed Long. Miss Anh even had a small Honda motorbike and took Long for rides on it. Sometimes they went to the market to shop. He still thought the market was a treat—although now when he went, his stomach didn't rumble with hunger.

One of the best things Miss Anh did was take him to his first-ever movie—*King Kong*. Long was on the edge of his seat the entire time, so excited he could hardly sit still. He stared in wonder as the lights started to go down and he saw the first flickers of color on the screen, then screamed with delight and dread, clutching Miss Anh's arm whenever the huge ape made an appearance. When the movie was over, Long begged to see it again, but Miss Anh had no more money for tickets. She told him he would be able to see lots of movies in America.

That fall of 1973, Amy left to join her new family in California. She promised to write. The other children were happy for her, but envious too. Long started wishing for three things: a new mother, a new family, a new home in America.

Still, his mother and especially his grandmother were always in his thoughts. Six months had passed since Ba brought him to Holt. Had she forgotten him? Was she okay? Why hadn't she come to visit?

Then, one afternoon, when he had just finished his studies on the rooftop and was going outside to play, he spotted her coming into the building. He ran to her, and she opened her arms to him, hugging him tight. For the next two hours, until she had to leave in order to be home by dark, the two of them walked around the area and then sat on the bench outside the Holt office. Ba told him she had to work every day of the week just to support herself, and it still wasn't enough. She did not want to return to the village, for she felt safer in the city and she wanted to stay closer to him.

When she left, she promised to return as soon as she could. As it turned out, this was not until the following spring. By then, Long had been at Holt a year and, in May 1974, had turned eight years old. This time, when Ba came to visit, she brought him his favorite meat sandwich. He could tell by how thin she was that she was not getting enough to eat, and he urged her to keep the sandwich for herself or at least share it. She would not hear of it, and was not satisfied until he had downed the whole thing.

They sat on a bench near the playground and talked. She said she was pleased at how much he had grown. She patted his arm. "They feed you well." She grinned, showing her dark teeth.

"I've been here many months, Ba."

"They say to find a home for a boy like you, it takes time. I hope it is soon."

"But when I go, it will probably be to America, and you won't see me anymore."

The smile vanished from her face, and Long was immediately sorry he had said this. He took a deep breath. "I could come home with you and find a job and help out. Then we could stay together."

Her faded eyes stared into the distance. Her hair was completely white now, and her hands more withered than before. "There is nothing for a small child. And I have no extra rice."

When she said goodbye and started her long walk back home, he stood at the gate and waved as long as he could see her.

Once again, sadness engulfed him, swirling around the hole in his heart. Why hadn't his mother stayed alive to care for him? Why couldn't he stay with Ba? Would he ever have a family? Where did he belong?

He did not go back into the Center for several minutes. He didn't want the other children to see his tears.

A FAMILY FOR LONG

Late one fall day in 1974, as Long played with a group of children on the playground, he saw Ky hurrying toward them, a big smile on his face. "I'm going to be adopted!" Ky blurted out. "They just told me. A family in Canada chose me. My new name is David."

The children gathered around him, sharing his excitement. They repeated his new name over and over, commenting on how odd it sounded. Long joined in. He was happy for his friend, but he wished he were the one making the announcement.

In school, Long worked hard at learning English. He mastered words and phrases like "hello" and "thank you," and sentences like "I am hungry" and "I am happy to meet you." In December, the teachers decided the children would put on a Christmas program for all the staff and invited guests. Long learned to do a special dance and to sing carols like "Silent Night." He took the singing very seriously. If Americans sang these songs, then he wanted to learn them.

A Christmas card arrived for the children from Amy. She described her new home, with its swimming pool, fireplace, and playroom. The children were wide-eyed with wonder as they read the card. Why did one family need its own swimming pool? And what was a fireplace? Was it a place where you cooked food?

On a rainy afternoon a few weeks later, Long was called to the office. He left class, his heart beating hard. Maybe his grandmother had come to visit.

He had not seen her in many months. Or maybe . . . But he couldn't even hope for that.

A social worker greeted him and offered him a chair. He sat down as she studied some papers on her desk. She looked up. "I have some good news for you, Long."

He held his breath, trying to concentrate on what she was saying. Then he heard the words, "We have a family who would like to adopt you."

Long thought his ears must be playing tricks on him. But she repeated her words, assuring him it was so. "They live in a little town called West Liberty, Ohio, and it's you they want. I think we can have all the paperwork done in time for you to leave next June."

Long's heart was pounding so hard, he could hardly hear his own voice when he asked in a whisper, "Do I have a new name?"

"You do. It's Matthew. They want to call you Matt."

Matt. Another strange American name. He thought for a moment. He had always been Long. Could he become someone else?

Matthew. Matt.

Finally he took a breath. "That will be okay," he said.

And then he smiled.

~

The family that had chosen Long was the Steiners. Jim Steiner was a doctor. His wife, Mary, was a homemaker. They had three sons: Dan, age seventeen, Doug, fifteen, and Jeff, thirteen.

For two years the Steiners had been working their way through all the application forms and paperwork to adopt a Vietnamese orphan. Back in 1960 the Steiners had lived in South Vietnam for six months. Jim had worked as a missionary doctor with people suffering from leprosy—a horrible, disfiguring disease. When Mary gave birth to their son Doug at the leprosarium hospital, Jim was the doctor.

The Steiners loved the people and culture of South Vietnam. But they knew life there was especially hard for Amerasian orphans and that as these children grew older, they often suffered increasing discrimination. Sometimes such children were called "half-breed" and treated poorly. Jim and Mary felt they could offer a home to one of them. Because the Steiner boys were in their teens, they decided to request an older child.

Long, in the photo sent to the Steiners

The Holt Foundation had sent them a photo of Long. "He looked kind of sad, like a little boy we wanted to help," says Mary Steiner. "Our hearts went out to him. We couldn't choose anyone else."

Through the months of January, February, and March 1975, the Steiners got to know Long through letters and photos. They told him about Ohio—that it was in the middle of the United States and had lots of trees and rolling hills. They said they lived in the country, where there was plenty of space to play. With Miss Anh's help, Long wrote back a few sentences in English and enclosed some drawings.

He often studied the family photo they sent him, memorizing each one of the Steiners. His eyes always went first to the mother. In the photo, she had short, curly brown hair, glasses, and a shy smile. She looked kind. Then he studied Dan, Doug, and Jeff, wondering what it would be like to have three brothers. It could be fun—older boys to play with.

Long had mixed feelings about the father in the photo. He looked nice, but could Long trust that? His own father had left him when he was still a baby. His stepfather had been cruel. Besides, if you had a mother, why would you need a father?

Having a father *sounded* nice. Maybe, just maybe, this time it would work out.

~

But as Long dreamed of his new family and the life he would have in America, the Vietnam War suddenly roared to life. In January 1975, the Communist army of North Vietnam began a major offensive against the South. To their surprise, they met little of the resistance that had stopped them in the past. Though some South Vietnamese army units fought back bravely, many others were fearful that they could not win because they no longer had American troops to assist them, so they did not try. Some South Vietnamese soldiers abandoned their military posts and went home to their families.

Suddenly everything was happening swiftly—so swiftly that all of South Vietnam was thrown into a state of panic. Each day came word that

another city or province had fallen to the Communists. The North Vietnamese soldiers were ruthless, killing both soldiers and civilians in their
path. Within weeks, the North Vietnamese controlled important strategic
areas in South Vietnam and continued to push southward.

Instead of taking a stand, the president of South Vietnam ordered his
troops to fall back to the Saigon region to defend the city and outlying areas. The retreat turned into a rush for safety. As frantic soldiers fled toward
Saigon, so did hundreds of thousands of refugees, jamming roads, disrupt-
ing the military, and creating a withdrawal that became known as the Con-
voy of Tears.

Pursuing them was the army of North Vietnam.

*Carrying her wounded child, a woman and other refugees flee from heavy
fighting north of Saigon in 1975*

No Way Out

By the end of March 1975, the war had reached Saigon. The North Vietnamese troops were still miles away, but they had the city surrounded. Soon they would break through the last South Vietnamese military resistance and march into the streets.

Within the city, everything had changed. People feared for their lives. The Communist takeover of Danang, the second largest city in South Vietnam, had been bloody and brutal. Many children were killed alongside their parents, most of them while trying to flee. The actual taking of Saigon could be worse. The Communists were sure to single out foreigners, especially Americans, and anyone who had worked for them. They would also target South Vietnamese soldiers, government officials, and their families. This meant hundreds of thousands of people were in danger, and with the city surrounded, there were only two ways out: by sea and by air.

To try to escape by sea was especially dangerous. Those who were desperate enough to try it had to motor or row small boats forty-five miles along the Saigon River past enemy troops and then out into the South China Sea. There, large ocean vessels, including American military ships, would pick up the lucky ones. The rest faced the open ocean as they tried to get to a distant, friendly port. Along the way, they could encounter pirates, who would rob and might murder them, as well as storms, sharks, and the blazing sun.

Some 17,000 South Vietnamese refugees crowd the deck of the SS Pioneer Contender *trying to escape the war*

By air was the best way out. But every seat on every outgoing commercial flight was booked. Desperate people jammed the offices of the airlines, begging anyone going in or coming out to help them. No amount of money could buy a seat.

From positions just miles outside the city, the North Vietnamese army began to fire randomly at the airport. Because of the extreme danger, commercial airlines stopped their regular flights. The only planes still landing and taking off at Tan Son Nhut Airport were private charter planes or military flights.

People looked to the U.S. government for help. Would it send last-minute aid, perhaps preventing a takeover? Would it undertake a massive evacuation of all the South Vietnamese who had worked for and helped Americans? Or would it leave these people to their fate? No one knew.

~

At Holt, Long knew something was about to happen. All the older kids did. Their teachers tried to keep routines normal, but the children saw the concern on the adults' faces, the sudden tears, and the increased activity at the Center.

At first Long didn't worry. The war had been going on since before he was born. If there were a serious problem, America would come to South Vietnam's defense. He was certain of that. Besides, he was going to leave in three to four months for his new home in America. Ky had already gone.

Then he overheard Lan, one of Holt's Vietnamese staff members, talking to another staff member.

"I try to stay calm," she said softly, "but will the streets run with blood when the Communists arrive? I hear they will kill anyone with connections to foreigners."

"That's just a rumor," the staff member protested. "Nobody knows."

"It has happened other places. They could punish me because I work for Americans or because my child's father was an American soldier. They might hurt my little Tai for being half American."

"Can her father help you?"

Lan shook her head. "I don't know where he is. How can I save my daughter?"

As Long listened, he became frightened. He was Amerasian, too! Would the Communists try to hurt *him*?

The next day, Long and some of the other children witnessed a chilling sight. While they were playing outside, several mothers holding small children came to the gate of the wall that surrounded the playground and the

Holt Center. They pleaded with staff to take their children and keep them safe. "You must get my baby to America!" cried one. "My family lived under the Communists in the North. He must not grow up that way." Another tried to reach through the gate to grab a staff member's arm. "When the Communists come, I will kill myself," she sobbed, "but please save my child!"

A young mother with her child seeks help from Holt

Miss Anh immediately moved the children away so they could not watch, but Long had seen and heard enough to suddenly realize how serious the war situation had become. But surely the American people would not let down the people of South Vietnam in their greatest hour of need.

What Long did not know was that in America, many people were pressuring the government to resist offering additional support to South Vietnam. For ten years, the United States had tried to help South Vietnam win the war. More than 58,000 American soldiers had already died in what the Vietnamese often referred to as the American War, and the Americans had finally withdrawn. The Vietnam War had created a rift in American society that would take decades to heal. The U.S. Congress was not going to vote any last-minute aid. This time, South Vietnam was on its own.

In Saigon, this was not yet known. At Holt's Saigon Center, staff members listened constantly to the American news station, trying to get the latest war information. Holt had already evacuated forty children from its care center in Danang before that city fell to the Communists. Those children and some from the Saigon center had left earlier when commercial flights were still available. But Holt had more than four hundred children still in Saigon. Most were Amerasian, and almost all of them were already assigned to adoptive families in other countries. No one questioned the necessity of getting the children out of the country. Under the Communist regime that would soon govern South Vietnam, their lives could be difficult, for in them flowed "the blood of the enemy."

There was another problem. During the transition to a new Communist government, who would care for the children? The Vietnamese staff would not dare come to work, for that would reveal their association with Americans, leaving the children with little or no care. Although Long was healthy, many of the children were not. Some had been crippled by disease or war injuries and needed braces, crutches, or daily physical therapy. Many, many children needed daily medication. It was painfully clear that their very survival depended on getting as quickly as possible to families that could look after their needs.

~

As the days passed, the American staff at Holt frantically tried to locate a privately chartered plane to airlift the children to safety. Every day they

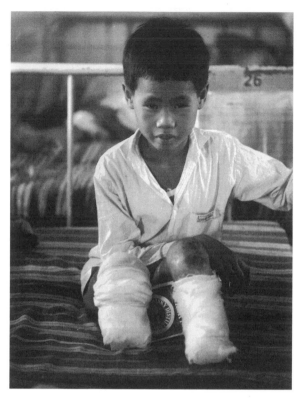

This boy, one of many civilian victims of the fighting between the Vietcong and the Allied forces, lost both legs when he was caught in the middle of intense street fighting in Saigon

talked to Holt staff in Oregon. Had they found a plane yet? Did they have any possibilities? As March turned into April, the situation in Saigon grew worse. Food prices escalated. Milk for the children was scarce. It was harder to get some supplies, impossible to get others. The North Vietnamese shelled the airport more frequently, increasing fears it would have to be shut down—and then *nobody* would get out. The American embassy checked daily on the Americans still in Saigon, but the U.S. government had not yet ordered an evacuation.

Each night on the roof of the Holt Center, staff members saw more flares and heard more gunfire. In the streets, new blockades and checkpoints sprang up overnight. In spite of the South Vietnamese government's attempts to keep refugees from overwhelming the city, they still crowded in, hungry and afraid. The population had not yet panicked, but everyone was on edge, waiting for the worst.

Just when it seemed that nerves would snap from tension, Holt's American director, Bob Chamness, received the phone call he had been waiting for. "We've found a plane!" he shouted excitedly to the others. "We're going to get *all* the children out!"

The phone call was from the Holt office in Oregon. They had arranged with Pan American Airlines to send a 747 jumbo jet that would hold more than four hundred children and adults. For the nonprofit Holt agency, the cost was a fortune: almost $250,000—which included very expensive insurance required by Pan Am for setting down a plane in a war zone. A private donor had agreed to loan the money. The scheduled arrival and takeoff date was April 5—just two days away.

There was no time to celebrate. So much still needed to be done. The staff dived into the job of readying everything for the children to leave. They needed to prepare formula, food, diapers, clothes, and medicine. They had to set up an intensive-care hospital unit on the plane for sick and malnourished children. Some of these children would need to be hooked up to IVs or other medical equipment during the long flight.

One of the biggest worries was making sure the two hundred Holt babies staying with foster parents in the Saigon area were ready to go on the flight. Social workers had to contact each family, none of whom had telephones, and tell them to have their foster child at the Holt Center early on the morning of April 5.

Gathering the necessary paperwork for each child was a huge task. Under the best of circumstances, processing the children for their trips abroad was difficult and time-consuming. Each one had to have a birth certificate, a wrist identification band, a passport, and emergency travel documents. All the children needed exit visas, which had to be issued by the South Vietnamese government. How could they get those when that very government was collapsing?

Six other child assistance groups were also trying to get their children out of the country, and all of them also needed government permission. The agencies petitioned Vietnamese officials with letters and used whatever contacts they had. Fortunately, the minister of welfare understood their plight and realized they were saving children's lives. He granted blanket permission for all the orphaned children to leave.

Then, as the Holt staff worked feverishly, determined to be ready for the April 5 flight, they received an amazing offer.

"We got a call from the American embassy telling us that President Gerald Ford had decided the government would assist with the evacuation," says John Williams, one of the Holt administrators in Saigon. "The press had already dubbed this effort Operation Babylift. We did not know how many planes there would be, but we were offered the first plane, at no cost to us."

The Holt American staff agonized over what to do. In the end, they decided to turn down the government's offer. "We had the Pan Am flight all arranged and could take all our children with us on that flight. We would have to leave 180 behind if we accepted the use of the government's military cargo plane," John says. "In spite of the cost, we felt that the Pan Am plane was the right choice for us."

Long could not know at the time that this decision would save the lives of many of Holt's children—including, perhaps, his own.

THE CRASH OF THE C-5A

When Long found out he would leave in just two days to go to his new family, he was filled with mixed emotions. He *wanted* to go, and he was worried about the war, but he was not going to have a chance to say good-bye to Ba, and that was very hard.

April 4, his last day in Saigon, was so hot and humid that the children did not go to the roof. Instead, they did their studies inside. The staff kept them there for another reason as well: the airport was being shelled and they could see fires when they looked in that direction from the roof.

As Long worked on his studies that day and thought about his grand-mother, he was unaware of a tragedy unfolding nearby. Rosemary Taylor and her organization, Friends For All Children, had accepted the govern-ment's offer of the first evacuation flight. Like Holt, FFAC had been search-ing for a way to get the children in its care out of the country. Many of these children had serious medical conditions, and the FFAC staff was de-termined to evacuate as many of them as possible. The military plane would be a start.

In the sweltering heat of April 4, the FFAC staff put 230 orphans and fifty adult escorts onto a C-5A cargo plane supplied by the American gov-ernment. Security at Tan Son Nhut Airport was very tight. Not only was there fear of attack by the North Vietnamese; there was also the threat that South Vietnamese who were frantic to get out of the country might try to take over the plane.

The loading of passengers had to be done as quickly as possible. The babies were strapped into seats on the upper deck of the huge aircraft. In the open cargo space below, normally used to transport helicopters, adult escorts did their best to secure the children on the floor. Some of the children clutched teddy bears or photos of their adoptive families. The older children understood what was happening and were proud and excited that they were going to their new homes. They shyly waved goodbye to staff staying behind, and set off for their new lives.

The gigantic plane with its precious cargo lumbered down the runway and lifted into the sky. But then, something terrible happened. Fifteen minutes after takeoff, as the plane neared the ocean and the first leg of its journey to America, an explosion suddenly rocked the aircraft. It immediately began losing altitude. As the pilot struggled to return the badly crippled plane to the airport, the adults aboard scrambled to administer oxygen to the children. But there were too few oxygen masks, and most of them did not work.

The plane crashed into a rice paddy, just a few miles from the airport runway. It hit with such force that pieces of the plane began to break apart. It shuddered, then seemed to bounce back into the air before it struck the ground again, lurching and bouncing through the watery muck. The noise was deafening—screeching, high-pitched, and jarring. Finally the plane came to a stop, a heap of burning wreckage mired in swampy ground, with black smoke belching into the air from burning fuel.

Most of the adults on board were killed. Miraculously, 152 of the 230 children aboard survived, though dozens had burns, broken bones, and other serious injuries. Many would later suffer from learning disabilities and other problems because they did not get enough oxygen during the crash. Emotional problems would plague some of them, as well as some of the adults who had cared for them or who tried to assist them later.

South Vietnamese soldiers stand in the middle of the wreckage of the first Operation Babylift flight, which crashed shortly after takeoff on April 4, 1975

~

Word that a planeload of orphans had crashed while escaping Saigon be-came headline news around the world. In Saigon, residents saw the smoke rising near the airport and heard the nonstop sirens racing to the scene to rush victims to the hospital. On the streets, rumors quickly spread that the plane had been shot down and everyone aboard killed. Later it was learned that the rear cargo doors had blown off because of a mechanical malfunction.

The horror of what had happened stunned everyone. "The crash of the C-5A . . . It could have been us and our children," says Glen Noteboom, who supervised Holt's Vietnamese social workers. "How could we even contemplate such a horror? Our hearts were heavy with grief for all those innocent children and adults, yet we had to keep on preparing everything for our flight the next morning.

"It was like the city of Saigon was dying, like the whole country was dying."

~

Long did not hear the crash, but he learned about it a short time later. He was supposed to leave on his flight the next morning. Now he wondered, would he be brave enough to get on the airplane?

Late that afternoon he was told he had a visitor. He ran to the office, hardly daring to wish that it could be Ba.

There she stood. When Ba saw her beloved grandson, she burst into sobs. Gathering him in her arms, she cried, "I thought you were dead! I thought you were dead! They told me all the children died."

Tears rolled down Long's cheeks. He had thought he would never see Ba again. Yes, he was alive, but now they were about to lose each other for good. He hugged his tiny, elderly grandmother tight, holding her close, knowing he was saying his final goodbye.

OPERATION BABYLIFT

The next morning, April 5, Long awoke with a start. He had slept fitfully, tossing and turning in the night, thinking about what was ahead of him. This was the day he would fly to America. It was really here!

He wanted to go. He wanted a new family, and he wanted to live in America. But there was also that worry he couldn't ignore. He was leaving so much here. He was leaving Ba.

Already the air was hazy and hot—even hotter than usual. He looked at the long pants, shirt, and sweater given to him to wear on the trip. He could not imagine needing warm clothing, but Miss Anh had told him it would be cold in the city called Chicago when his plane landed there. He decided to put on the clothes later, and stuck them in the small bag he would carry on the plane. Also in the bag were the letters he had received from the Steiners, a few miniature toy cars they had sent him, and their family photo. He wished he had a picture of his mother and grandmother. He would have to remember them in his mind, the same way he would remember Vietnam.

After breakfast, an American newspaper reporter who was visiting the Holt Center approached him. "I'm told you speak some English," the American said. "I'd like to interview you." Long agreed, doing the best he could to answer a series of questions.

One was "How do you feel about your trip today?" Long thought for a

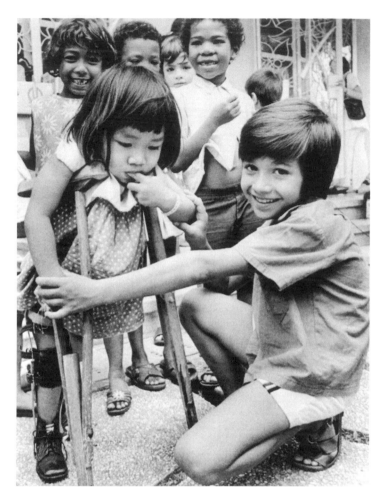

This photograph of Long saying goodbye to his friends at the Holt Center appeared in newspapers around the world

moment. "I am so happy to go to America," he replied. Then, looking at Miss Anh, he added that he was sorry to leave his teacher behind. At the end the reporter asked, "What will you say when you meet your new family?" Long struggled to express himself in English. Haltingly he said, "I am so happy to see you." Then he burst out, "At the airport!"

~

Early that morning, foster mothers and members of their families began gathering at the Holt Center, arriving by motorbike, public bus, or on foot. Holding the babies they had been caring for and were now giving up, many of the mothers were overcome with emotion. Their tears flowed easily.

Most of the Holt staff had been up all night, trying to complete the task of gathering documents and supplies for the children who would be leaving on the Pan American Airlines 747 jumbo jet. Of the four hundred children traveling on the plane, nearly three hundred were infants or toddlers. All but a dozen had adoptive families waiting for them in the United States, and those without adoptive families would soon have them.

By midmorning the first floor and courtyard play area were jammed with foster families and children. Because of the heat and confusion, most of the babies were crying. All that previous week parents and guardians had come to the Holt Center, asking the Americans to take their children along when they left the country. Staff members had to turn down such requests, making only a few exceptions for children who were Amerasian, had the proper paperwork to get out of the country, and had no parent or guardian who could care for them.

Long and the other older children going on the flight helped entertain the younger children, playing games with them on the playground. Long had changed into his new shirt and pants. They were so hot!

He was running an errand for one of the teachers when he heard Lan talking to one of the Americans. "We can take your daughter, Tai, with us," the American said to her. "She has the necessary paperwork, and we have a long list of approved families wishing to adopt our children. We'll find her a good home. But you must decide by noon. We have only a few spaces left on the flight."

Lan hid her face in her hands. "How can I live without my little daughter?"

The staff member's voice was full of sympathy. "I wish you could go, too, Lan," she said, "but after yesterday's crash, and the concern about sabotage at the airport, it's become almost impossible to help Vietnamese nationals like you get out of the country."

Long continued on his errand, troubled by what he had heard. Poor Lan! What would she do?

At noon, the buses for the airport began arriving to pick up the children and the fifty escorts who would care for them on the flight. Escorts had been recruited from the community of Americans living in Saigon who wanted to return to the United States.

The children were lined up, and one more time, names were checked against a list. The air was filled with the wailing of foster mothers as they touched their babies for the last time. As the first bus started to leave, a foster mother tried to pull herself up on the wire mesh covering the bus windows, hoping for one last glimpse of the baby she had cared for. Someone pulled her away, and other mothers moved close to comfort her.

Long was in line to get on the next bus. His teacher, Miss Anh, came over to say her final goodbye.

"Will you be okay?" he asked anxiously. He saw her lips tremble, but she said brightly, "No need to worry about me. My family is here, and we will be fine. You have a good life in America."

They hugged one last time. As Miss Anh moved away, Long saw Lan leading four-year-old Tai. She was whispering something to the little girl. Tai looked confused, but she did not cry.

Stopping by Long, Lan bent down to her daughter. "This is Long," she said softly. "He is going on the plane, too, just like you."

Long tried to smile reassuringly at the little girl, and he waved to her as Lan helped her find a place at the back of the line. He thought he had never seen a face look as sad as Lan's.

Suddenly it was his turn to board the bus. He slid into a seat and scrunched himself against the window to make room for an American woman he didn't know, who had two small children on her lap. He wished Miss Anh were coming to America. Parting from her was another goodbye, and it left him with that familiar feeling of emptiness.

It was very hot in the strong noonday sun, and the bus was so jammed with babies, children, and adults, that Long felt he was gasping for breath. Finally they began to move. This was it. He was on his way! He tried to catch a final glimpse of the Holt Center and his teacher, but he was on the wrong side of the bus, and could see nothing.

He looked out at passing traffic. Somewhere in Saigon was his grandmother, but he knew she was a long way in the other direction. He didn't want to think about her, so he watched people on the street instead. He had already overheard enough adult conversations to know they were worried that someone might try to stop the bus or take it over. The adults were grim-faced. Long could feel the tension.

The bus inched along through the dense traffic. People were everywhere, more people than ever before. He wondered where they were all going. Was there actually anywhere to go?

When the bus finally arrived at the airport gate, guards ordered it to stop. Long knew that getting through the gates was a big worry for the Holt officials. The guards didn't have to let them through. Almost afraid to breathe, Long watched as the guards came aboard the bus. They wore army uniforms, and their guns were ready at their sides. In loud voices they demanded to see the official documents for the passengers. They studied the papers while babies screamed in the stifling heat. Long wondered why everything was taking so long. When would the bus start to move again? Through the window, he saw a crowd of Vietnamese outside the airport gates. Most held on to suitcases. They watched the bus silently. Long thought they must know that no one on the bus could help them.

Finally the guards were satisfied. As they got off the bus, Long realized he'd been holding his breath. The guards waved the bus through the gates, directing it onto the open tarmac. Armed soldiers were everywhere. From his window, Long saw a thin trail of smoke in the distance. Someone said it was from the crash of the C-5A the day before, and Long felt his stomach tighten.

Slowly the bus made its way toward the gigantic airplane that stood waiting. Long could not believe its size. It was as tall as a three-story building. How would it ever get off the ground? How could it stay up in the air?

The moment the bus stopped next to the plane, the adults sprang into action. They carried the small children and directed the older ones. *"Hurry, hurry, hurry!"* Everyone understood the urgency, for danger from incoming fire was all around them. Small children were handed to waiting adults and whisked aboard the plane. When it was Long's turn, he moved as quickly as he could, down the bus steps, then up the steps into the plane, guided by adults talking so fast in nonstop English that he couldn't follow what they were saying.

Once inside the plane, he didn't even have time to look around before an adult pointed him toward a row where he should sit. He moved into the seat next to the window, glad to be out of the way. It was even hotter inside the plane than it had been on the bus. Long's clothes were damp and sticking to him. The air-conditioning could not come on until the plane lifted into the air.

Adults worked quickly to get the children aboard. One of them asked Long to assist. He left his bag on his seat and helped settle the small children in the rows right around him. Working with the babies was hard because they wiggled so much. The tiniest ones were in bassinets the flight crew strapped securely into the seats.

Long's face was wet with sweat. All through the plane, babies screamed at the top of their lungs, adding to the chaos and confusion. He wished

Volunteers help settle children before takeoff aboard one of the military cargo planes that participated in Operation Babylift

they wouldn't cry so much. But you couldn't reason with babies. All you could do was try to soothe them. Long had better luck with children who were a little older. Most of the adults working around him spoke English, but Long knew the children were used to Vietnamese. "Don't worry," he assured them in their own language. "Soon we'll be in America, and you will have a new family, and you will be happy."

Holt staff, escorts, and the flight crew hurried through the aisle, trying to get everyone in a seat so the plane could take off. They counted the children, and then counted again. Long knew they were worried the enemy would start shelling the airport. He was too. *Hurry, hurry!*

More buses arrived, more children and adults. He saw Tai come on board and waved to her, but she didn't notice him. She was taken clear to the front of the airplane. Over and over the children were counted. Finally the counting stopped and Long returned to his seat and settled in. It was really going to happen! He was going to America!

The view from his window was one of the gigantic wings. As he looked at it, he suddenly realized that enemy soldiers could climb right onto it and break the windows and get in! What should he do?

The sound of the engines revving up startled him. It was so loud, he put his hands over his ears. Frightened by the noise, several children around him became hysterical. Escorts tried to comfort them. Suddenly, the wing flaps began to drop. To Long it looked as if the wing was broken. That meant the plane was like a bird with a broken wing, and it would crash, just like the plane did yesterday! He tried to swallow his fear, but his heart was beating hard. Maybe he should tell the pilot. No, he would be watchful. If it looked like the plane couldn't fly, he would let the pilot know.

When the plane started to taxi down the runway, Long held his breath and tightly gripped the arms of his seat. He kept an eye on the ground outside, watching to make sure enemy soldiers didn't start to throw grenades or fire rockets or storm across the tarmac to capture the plane.

The huge jet began to lift into the air. The angle of takeoff was so sharp that Long felt blood rush to his head. The skin on his face felt pulled and taut. It was almost as though he was lying on his back. Now even the crying children grew quiet.

Long thought his ears would explode. The roar of the plane was so loud, he couldn't hear anything else. Finally the plane began to level out. For a moment everyone on board was silent. Then, as if on cue, the adults broke out in spontaneous cheering. "We're safe now," someone said. "God bless the Vietnamese people, and God bless America," someone else said. Through his window, Long checked the wing. No enemy soldiers. No one trying to get in. They were safe!

As he joined the cheering around him, he realized he hadn't been the only one to feel afraid. Now he could smile again. He was leaving a land of war and heading to a land of promise and peace.

When the air-conditioning system finally began to fill the cabin with cooling air, Long heard adults sighing with relief. Then they were on their feet and immediately busy, tending to all the babies, who needed to be fed and changed and comforted.

Long looked out the window at the lush green country falling away far below. In spite of his excitement that he was going to America, he knew he was leaving behind all he had ever known.

He closed his eyes, trying to imagine his mother and Ba wrapping their arms around him and telling him everything would be okay. If only they could be with him.

He caught one last glimpse of his homeland, and then clouds covered everything. He took the photo of his new family from his bag and slowly, one at a time, touched the five faces looking back at him.

In a country far away, they were waiting for him. They were his future.

THE FLIGHT TO FREEDOM

Long would learn much later that the giant Pan Am 747 was almost the length of a football field. The crew had stocked the airplane with diapers, formula, milk, and changes of clothing for their youngest passengers. There were even coloring books, crayons, and other art supplies to entertain the older children. The galley was ready to serve everyone hamburgers when it was mealtime.

The flight carried 409 children and sixty adults. To care for all the children, the escorts had divided up the rows, and they spent the entire sixteen-hour flight attending to the children's needs.

"Fortunately, older children like Long could look out for themselves," says John Williams, the Holt administrator who was on the plane. "I was caring for ten babies by myself, with an occasional assist from the flight crew, so there was rarely a moment's rest. But it was happy work. We were so relieved to be on our way and to have all the children with us, though we were very distressed by what was happening back in Saigon."

Mostly, Long stayed in his seat because the aisle, which had thick red carpet, was always congested with staff and escorts rushing back and forth. Once a flight attendant took him on a brief visit to the luxurious upstairs lounge, where normally passengers could dine at tables set with linen cloths. For this special Operation Babylift flight, it had been turned into an intensive care medical unit. Volunteer doctors and nurses attended to the many children who were sick or who needed special hydration during the trip. All the medical equipment amazed Long. Isolettes held babies hooked up to tubes and machines. One toddler had a broken leg, and an older child was being treated for a severe burn.

Back in his seat, Long passed the time playing with his toy cars and making art projects for his new parents with the supplies given to him. He tried to sleep, but felt too excited. Besides, it was so noisy on the plane that he could hardly think, much less sleep. All those babies and all that crying! At any time, so many of them were wet, hungry, or just wanted to be held.

After five hours in the air, the plane landed on the island of Guam, in the Pacific Ocean, to refuel and change crews. When the governor of Guam came on board to greet them, the Holt officials realized for the first time what big news Operation Babylift had become. Everyone in the world, it seemed, was interested in the children and was concerned about their safe evacuation from Saigon.

The crash of the C-5A focused the world's attention on the plight of the orphaned children of South Vietnam. In the United States, adoption agencies—whether or not they had any connection with overseas adoption—were flooded with calls. Not understanding that nearly every child was spoken for, good-hearted people stepped forward to help, offering to take the children. A toll-free number was set up in Washington, D.C., to handle the inquiries. At times, more than a thousand calls a minute were turned away by busy signals.

Three other flights also left the same day as Long's—another chartered Pan Am jumbo jet and two military transport planes. Together the four planes carried nearly nine hundred children to new lives in the United States. Forty of the children were survivors of the C-5A crash the day before. Another 263 children left Saigon that same day bound for Canada and Australia. By the time Operation Babylift ended, 2,242 children would be

An airman and a volunteer help children aboard a plane that will deliver them to their waiting adoptive families

airlifted from Saigon as part of the U.S. government's pledge that all the orphans with homes already waiting for them would be evacuated from Saigon. It was the first time in history that the U.S. government had participated in such a project, working alongside agencies like Holt. The Holt Pan Am 747, with Long aboard, brought out Operation Babylift's single largest group of children.

~

As the plane sped on, cruising at a speed of 580 miles per hour, the Steiner family of West Liberty, Ohio, was traveling to O'Hare International Airport in Chicago, Illinois, to meet it. Although Long could not know it, he was a celebrity. When the interview conducted with him the morning of April 5 at the Holt Center appeared in newspapers across America, the Steiners' phone started ringing.

"How can my wife and I get one of those kids?" asked a typical caller. Jim or Mary then explained the adoption process, that they had been working two years on this, that much paperwork was required on both sides of the ocean. "But don't they have extra kids?" the caller would insist. "We'll take one." And again the Steiners would try to explain how international adoption worked.

"Holt had advised us to keep things as quiet and calm in the family as we possibly could, so when Long arrived, he would have time to adjust," Mary says. "But we were bombarded by people wanting to know how to adopt, and also by the press wanting to do stories on us. It was crazy."

Oldest son Dan had to work, so he didn't accompany his dad, mom, and brothers Doug and Jeff to Chicago. They arrived at the airport two hours before the plane was scheduled to land. About a dozen other families were also waiting—and so was the press.

"I was so excited at the time that nothing could bother me, not even all the reporters," Mary remembers. "I wasn't concerned about whether we would recognize our new son. I just knew we would. All I wanted was for that plane to hurry up and land."

~

After refueling in Guam, Long's plane stopped in Hawaii, the final destination for several children. The next stop was Seattle, Washington, where the children destined for West Coast homes departed the plane. That left two more stops: Chicago for the Midwest children, and New York City for the East Coast children.

Long thought his journey to America would never be over. On the flight from Seattle to Chicago, he grew restless. The plane was only half full because so many children had gotten off in Seattle. The last two hours of his trip, no longer interested in his toys or coloring or looking out the window, he took out the photo of the Steiners again. He wondered why they wanted another child when they already had three sons. How different would he look from these boys? Would they like him? He practiced his English: "I am so happy to meet you." "Hello." "Thank you." "I am hungry."

When the huge jet finally touched down in Chicago, Long unbuckled his seat belt the first moment possible, even though he knew he had to wait in his seat until all his documents were checked again and he could be escorted off the plane. He tried to be patient. Couldn't they hurry up? Why did everything take so long!

After what seemed like forever, he was told to come to the front of the plane. He had to force himself not to run.

A Holt staff member walked with him into the airport terminal. A bank of bright lights from all the news crews waiting for the children suddenly blinded him. He heard cries of excitement on either side of him, and two small children ahead of him were scooped into the arms of their new families.

He searched the waiting crowd. What if the Steiners had changed their minds and didn't come? What if they had decided they didn't want him?

And then he saw them. He knew those faces by heart. The man and the boys reached for him, but he saw only her.

In one movement, he rushed into the arms of his new mother, and the two of them held each other so close that anyone watching them knew they would never let go again.

INTO THE EYE OF THE STORM

Long was safe in the United States. But in Saigon, no one was safe. The North Vietnamese army was closing in on every side.

Fear gripped the city. When the Communists arrived, who would they single out to punish? How hard would life be after the takeover? Rumors spread that whole families were choosing to commit suicide together rather than live under Communist rule.

Three days after John Williams and Glen Noteboom flew to the United States as escorts on the plane transporting the Holt children, they returned to Saigon. They still had work to do. Bob Chamness met them at the airport.

"We knew the danger of returning, but since our April 5 flight, thirty more children had come into Holt's care," John says. "We also had several children who had remained behind because they were too sick to travel on that flight. We were determined to evacuate all these children."

John and Glen were surprised at how much Saigon had changed in just three days. At the airport gates they saw desperate Vietnamese begging and bribing the guards, hoping that once inside, they could get on a departing military cargo plane. The guards' uniforms were stuffed with money. People with nowhere else to go jammed the streets, making it difficult to get anywhere. Barbed-wire blockades and checkpoints were everywhere, though no one really knew why.

At the Holt Center, a few Vietnamese staff members still reported for work. Most of the children in their care were Amerasians. They had been brought to Holt either by members of religious orders who ran area orphanages or by frantic parents certain that Communists would mistreat or even kill them because they were half American.

John, Bob, and Glen assessed the situation. During the war, many Americans had come to Saigon to work for the American embassy or for one of the companies doing business with the South Vietnamese government. Marines continued to guard the embassy. Americans still in the city awaited orders from the U.S. government to evacuate. Only a few American planes were still landing and taking off at the airport, but because of the U.S. government's involvement in Operation Babylift, the men hoped they could arrange passage for the remaining children.

They began checking every possibility, not knowing how much time they had. Two weeks at most. A Catholic priest approached them and said he represented a group of American families who wanted to adopt Vietnamese babies. He was trying to find children to take back to the States with him. He had a satchelful of money and was going from agency to agency, offering any price for a child.

"He dared to ask us to turn over some of our children to him. I'm usually easygoing, but I was blind with rage," John says. "These children were not for sale! We always tried first to help families find a way to keep their child. If we took a child into our custody, we did a careful home study on prospective adoptive parents before we approved them. We felt we owed this to our children.

"The priest couldn't understand why we wouldn't help him. But apparently a few desperate parents turned their children over to him—people were crazy with fear—because we heard a few days later that he had several children at the airport and was trying to get them on a plane. We also heard that U.S. embassy officials planned to stop him. I don't know what finally happened."

By late April, Holt had secured a flight for the thirty-three children in its care. Once they were safely on their way, everyone at Holt breathed more easily. Bob, John, and Glen now had to figure out how to evacuate the Vietnamese staff and their family members who wanted to leave—one hundred people in all.

The biggest hurdle was getting them past the guards and into the airport. The three Americans tried several times to drive staff members through the gates, but were always stopped. No Vietnamese were allowed to enter—at least not without paying heavy bribes. The Holt staff wouldn't do that.

The situation in Saigon was extremely perilous. North Vietnamese rockets made direct hits on the city, adding to the growing panic. The president of South Vietnam resigned and fled the country. When U.S. President Gerald Ford announced that the Vietnam War was "finished as far as America is concerned," he closed the door on additional military aid from the United States and sealed the fate of South Vietnam: it *would* fall to the North.

Even with the airport being shelled, crowds mobbed the gates, hoping to find a way out. Bob, Glen, and John tried everything they could think of to get their Vietnamese staff past the guards. With each attempt, they used different vehicles given to them by others fleeing the country.

Then it happened. One of the cars was allowed to pass through the gates.

"We realized it had diplomatic license plates," John says. "Working as quickly as we could, we made trip after trip with this one car, taking as many people as possible each time. We were always afraid we'd be stopped, but finally we had everyone on the base."

American marines directed the Holt Vietnamese staff and their family members to one of the few airport warehouses that still had space. The others were already overflowing with Vietnamese men, women, and children who were waiting for evacuation.

"We received assurance from American officials that our staff would get out," John says. "Bob, Glen, and I were told that we must leave immediately or risk losing American protection, so we boarded another flight. That was on April 27."

The men flew to Singapore, where they planned to catch a flight to America. But when they arrived in Singapore, a heartbreaking message awaited them. "For reasons we've never understood, someone from the U.S. embassy had showed up at the warehouse and made all our staff people get on buses. Unbelievably, they were taken *back* to the Holt Center. One of our staff members somehow managed to call our Oregon office, begging for help. But there was nothing anyone could do. Nothing."

Lan was with the staff members trapped in Saigon. Though she had lost her daughter, Tai, who had gone on the Babylift flight with Long, she hoped she could escape to safety and live somewhere in freedom. When she realized that the Holt group could not leave, she decided to try one last possibility. She knew an American living in Saigon who worked for an international firm. He had once told her to contact him if she ever needed help. She did not know if he was still in the city, but she put through a call to his office. Both electricity and phone service had become so undependable, she could hardly believe it when the call went through and the operator put the man on the line.

"I'll try to help," he said when she explained her plight. "My company has a private plane leaving tonight. Maybe I can pull some strings and get you on it, provided you can get into the airport. Go to my apartment immediately and wait for instructions."

It took Lan two hours to make her way through the mobbed streets. She found a note on the American's apartment door addressed to her, stating that she was to go to a nearby school, where a car would meet her. Only half believing this, she hurried to the school. Within minutes, a car pulled up. The driver verified her identity and told her to get in. Traffic on the main streets was at a standstill, but the driver knew the side streets and got to the airport. At the gate, the car was waved through without stopping. The driver told her to go inside the terminal and wait until she heard her name called. She had only one small suitcase and her travel documents with her. She had no food or water and did not know any of the people who packed the terminal waiting room. She found a place against a wall and stayed there. Everyone looked nervous and upset. Some paced around and some cried, especially when they heard explosions outside. Lan could see smoke and fires on the runways from the Communist shelling, which increased every hour.

At three A.M., after nearly nine hours of waiting, she heard her name called. She was rushed aboard a small plane. She collapsed into a seat, and moments later, the plane lifted into the air. Once the plane was out of range of the rockets bursting around them, she looked out a window. She could see fires burning all around the city.

"I did not even know where we were flying to," she says. "I had no family left in Vietnam, but I had no one anywhere else, either. When I realized I had escaped, I was overcome with both joy and sorrow. I was all alone. I no longer had my daughter or my country, and I did not know if I could stand to live in the world without them."

~

On April 29, the American embassy finally began Operation Frequent Wind, the official evacuation of Americans still in Saigon. When the American radio station played "White Christmas," followed by the announcement that "the temperature in Saigon is 105 degrees and rising," Americans knew to hurry to their assigned evacuation sites.

The streets of downtown Saigon were cluttered with abandoned cars, clothing, and suitcases dropped by desperate people still hoping to escape. Discarded uniforms of soldiers, who had deserted the South Vietnamese army and now were trying to blend in with the general population, littered the landscape. Rioting and looting were creating destruction throughout the city.

It had become too dangerous for planes to leave from the airport. Helicopters were the best way out. They could land on flat roofs and needed no runway to take off. One helicopter evacuation site was the roof of the Amer-

Desperate Vietnamese try to scale the fourteen-foot wall surrounding the U.S. Embassy, hoping to be evacuated by helicopter from the embassy roof

ican embassy. Frantic Vietnamese mobbed the walled embassy compound, begging to be evacuated. American marines had to beat them back or even threaten to shoot them so arriving Americans could get inside.

Americans, other foreign nationals, and select Vietnamese lucky enough to make it to the embassy roof were crammed into helicopters and flown to U.S. Navy aircraft carriers waiting miles away in the ocean. One after another, throughout the afternoon and evening of April 29, helicopters landed and took off from the embassy roof, filling the air with the *whup-whup-whup* sounds of their whirring blades.

~

On April 30, 1975, the world awoke to the news that South Vietnam had surrendered. The long war was over. Very early that morning, the last remaining American marines boarded the final helicopter, carrying with them the American flag that had flown over the embassy. The Americans were safely out of the city. Left behind were thousands and thousands of terrified Vietnamese who had counted on their American friends to take them along.

Several hours later, North Vietnamese tanks rolled through the silent streets of Saigon. Instead of a bloodbath, over the next few months, tens of thousands of South Vietnamese who had opposed the North were rounded up and sent to "re-education camps," where they suffered terrible hardships. Saigon was renamed Ho Chi Minh City in honor of the North's long-time revolutionary leader. A curtain of silence descended upon the newly reunited Vietnam, closing it off from the West.

~

Lan was taken to Clark Air Force Base, in the Philippines, then several weeks later was flown to Camp Pendleton, in California. Thousands of Vietnamese refugees were there, waiting for American sponsors who would help them start new lives in the United States. Still grieving for her daughter, Lan called the Holt office in Oregon to report that she had made it to the United States.

Then a miracle occurred. Lan learned that Holt had not yet placed Tai with an adoptive family. She was still in foster care.

"She's with a family in San Francisco," they told Lan. "She'll be waiting for you."

Lan will never forget the best moment of her life, when her plane landed in San Francisco in June 1975 and she ran to embrace her daughter, Tai—a heartbroken little girl, who, until that moment, had thought her mother was dead.

A REAL AMERICAN BOY

As soon as he met them, Long felt at home with the Steiners. They called him Matt. This took a while to get used to, but he willingly accepted it. The name Long would be part of his past. Now he was Matthew Ray Steiner, Matt for short.

His first night with the Steiners, he slept sixteen straight hours. When he awoke, he was famished. Mary Steiner said later that for the first few weeks, her new son's appetite was ravenous. She was a good cook, and because she had lived in both Thailand and Vietnam, she knew how to prepare foods Matt liked, though he still added hot sauce to everything.

To his surprise, he was a media celebrity. People already knew who he was because of the widely reprinted article by the reporter who had interviewed him at the Holt Center. Cards and letters from well-wishers all over the country began arriving at the Steiner home. Television and newspaper reporters came for interviews.

"Matt loved it," recalls his mother. "It was a little harder for Dan, Doug, and Jeff to see this new family member getting so much attention, but they were good sports."

Matt immediately took to his new brothers, especially Doug, who was fifteen. "He went out of his way for me," Matt says. "As soon as I arrived, he gave me a toy truck and played with me. He took me under his wing."

Ironically, it had been Doug who had voiced concerns about his parents adopting a child. "But Doug was born in South Vietnam and maybe that's why the two became close friends," Mary Steiner says.

Gradually Matt grew close to Dan and Jeff. "We had our ups and downs, as any brothers do," Matt says, "like the time Jeff said something that made me mad and I threw a sandwich at him, making a mess on the floor. We did stuff like that. But mostly we got along fine."

Long, now known as Matt, with his new family, the Steiners, two weeks after arriving in America

The Steiners thought Matt would know very little English and were surprised that he could handle simple communication. They also were surprised that he knew how to tie the shoelaces on his first pair of sneakers. Matt remembered the day his friend Ky had taught him this strange skill, and now he was glad that he had spent time learning it.

He eagerly wore the clothes they bought him, willing to do anything that made him look more American—though these clothes took some getting used to. "In Vietnam, I wore shorts and a shirt every day. I never wore underwear. Often I was barefoot. Now I had to wear shoes and socks and underwear, and then layer on a T-shirt, an outer shirt, a sweater, and finally a coat. I had never experienced cold weather, and had to get used to it. The first time I saw snow, I was excited and mystified. My mom explained that every flake had a unique pattern. I couldn't get over that. I spent a lot of time trying to catch the flakes so I could examine them."

The Steiners' home was average in size but seemed huge to Matt, who had always lived in small, crowded spaces. Until he could get used to being alone in his own bedroom at night, he shared a room with thirteen-year-old Jeff. That still wasn't enough company for Matt. For the first few nights, he found his way to his new parents' bedroom, wanting to sleep on the floor by them, only to have them gently steer him back to his own bed.

Then there was the family dog, Moose, a mix of German sheepdog and collie. The few small dogs Matt remembered from his mother's village were not pets and never went into anyone's house, but Moose went anywhere he wanted. And the moment he saw Matt, he bounded over, ready to play. Matt drew back in fear. Gradually he realized that the dog just wanted to bestow sloppy kisses on him. Before long, Matt and Moose were good friends.

Matt's new brothers loved sports. They were eager to introduce him to all sorts of outdoor activities, especially golf, which everyone in the family

Matt's new brothers, Dan, Doug, and Jeff, teach him how to play basketball

played. Within days of his arrival, Matt knew how to hold and swing a golf club. Soon he was an avid player, practicing his swing in the big yard surrounding the Steiners' house. That yard seemed vast to Matt, who was used to city streets and playing inside a walled courtyard. He grew to appreciate all the space once he mastered his brothers' three-wheeled motor scooter. This was better than a bicycle! He spent happy hours riding it, Moose running beside him.

His first trip into West Liberty, Ohio, was a revelation. Most of the fifteen hundred residents already knew who he was and called him by name. At the grocery store, Matt was wide-eyed. This was no Saigon street market. Instead of live ducks and chickens, meat was packaged in plastic and ready to cook. There weren't many fruits and vegetables, at least not by Vietnamese standards. Where were the mounds of rice and potatoes, and all the fresh fish? Where were the coconuts you could cut a hole into in order to sip creamy milk through a straw? And nobody bargained over prices. Americans just paid whatever the sticker demanded.

Having a mother again was the best part of Matt's new life. Before he started school, he spent all his time with her, going with her on errands and helping her around the house. Mary read to him and worked with him on his reading and spelling. She did everything she could to help him understand his new life.

Matt took his time getting to know his new father. Jim Steiner understood this need and did not push. He was a man devoted to his family and to the practice of medicine, giving of his skills to help others. He believed in living simply. He had an inquisitive mind, and he talked to Matt about everything going on in his new son's life. He always made it clear how proud he was of Matt. Over time, Matt learned to love his father deeply.

"One day Dad invited me to go jogging with him, something he did regularly," says Matt. "I became a runner and often went out with Dad. I prize those memories."

It didn't take Matt long to feel like a full member of the family. All the boys had assigned chores and also helped their mother in the kitchen, setting the table and doing dishes. Matt went with his parents to sports events to cheer on his brothers, who played on various teams at school.

Along with his immediate family, Matt acquired aunts, uncles, cousins, and two grandmothers. "Both grandmas were wonderful cooks, and I loved going to their homes to visit," Matt says. "Each of them accepted me, encouraged me, took a lot of interest in everything I was doing, and made me feel I was special to them."

They also reminded him of his grandmother back in Vietnam, and that made him feel sad. Where was Ba? What had happened to her? Matt had no address for her or any way to contact her. Often he thought about Ba when he went to church on Sundays. He remembered the gentle Buddhist prayers he had learned from Ba when she would take him to the temple to pray for his mother's soul. The Buddhist faith emphasized helping others, especially the poor and homeless. The Steiners were Mennonites, a Christian religion that stressed simplicity and service to others. Matt saw similarities between the two religions. He found comfort in the Steiners' faith and soon embraced it as his own.

When Matt arrived at the Steiner home in early April 1975, his new parents had decided that since there was only a little over a month left of school, Matt would stay home and Mary Steiner would tutor him. But Matt wanted to go to school right away. He was eager to learn and to get caught up on his studies. His desire was to be just like all the other kids. More than anything, Matt wished to be a real American boy.

His parents were unsure, but gave in. As soon as Matt arrived for his first day in third grade, he wondered if he'd made a mistake. He was eight years old and small and thin for his age. He did not speak English very well. He was behind in every subject. He knew several boys from church, but otherwise the children were strangers to him—yet they all knew his name because his picture had been in the paper.

At recess the first morning, the third grade girls formed a circle around him. They giggled and whispered to each other. Matt didn't understand what was going on and started to run. They chased after him. Then several boys surrounded him, running along with him, trying to keep the girls away.

"We ran and ran, all over the playground like that, the girls still chasing me. That was my introduction to American girls. In Vietnam, girls would never act like that. They were expected to be ladylike. So this was quite a shock to me."

In anticipation of Matt's ninth birthday on May 15, the Steiners planned a birthday party, complete with gifts and Matt's first-ever birthday cake. When the big day came, the avalanche of birthday cards that arrived in the mail surprised him. Dozens of people had saved the newspaper article about him, which mentioned his birth date, and they sent him cards. Among his gifts were a kite, a puzzle of the United States, and a baseball and glove. Matt could not believe these treasures now belonged to him. "I had been so poor in Vietnam," he says.

When school ended, the Steiners moved for a year to a little town on an Indian reservation in the Southwest where Dr. Steiner was volunteering as a medical missionary at the reservation health clinic. The family lived in a small home on the reservation, and Matt went to fourth grade there. In this new setting, he was no longer a celebrity. With his black hair and dark skin, he blended in with his Indian classmates. The teachers at the reservation school gave him lots of extra help with his studies. When the family returned to West Liberty and Matt started fifth grade, he had caught up with his classmates. He had also mastered English and was quickly forgetting how to speak Vietnamese.

Mostly, Matt's life moved along smoothly. He loved to learn and was an excellent student. He excelled in math. He grew and filled out. He lettered in football, golf, basketball, baseball, cross-country, and track. He enjoyed playing golf with his brothers and watching football on television. He played trumpet in the band. He helped out at home, and once he was old enough to work, he always had a part-time job. He went to church regularly and had a circle of friends, including girlfriends.

But, as happy as he was with his family, he still missed his birth mother and Ba. Sometimes he felt confused by everything that had happened. Why had his mother killed herself? Hadn't she loved him enough to want to stay alive? Wasn't he a good enough son? Couldn't Ba have found a way to keep

him? He didn't want to upset the Steiners with these concerns, so he kept
them to himself.

There were other rough spots. Every year, it seemed one or two boys
took it upon themselves to tease him, calling him "Chink," "gook," or
"Chinaman," and saying it in a way that conveyed prejudice and hate. Once
Matt got into a fight when a bully tried to provoke him by calling him

Matt (third from right) as a proud member of his school's baseball team

names. "I stood my ground with him," Matt says, "and he never bothered
me again."

Then came an incident that hurt deeply. In eighth grade during a football game, Matt made a successful block. When he reached the sidelines
and the congratulations of his teammates, one of them, an old friend, called
out, "Hey, Chink, good play!"

"It stopped me cold," Matt says. "I know he thought it was funny and
didn't realize how degraded I felt by it. I actually had tears in my eyes. I've

never forgotten it. When other kids called me names, it made me angry. But a friend . . . well, that really hurt.

"I knew I looked different from my family, but I didn't want to *be* different. I wanted to blend in. I tried to forget the Vietnamese part of me. I didn't want anything to do with it. I never stopped missing my birth mother and grandmother, but I did not want to go back to Vietnam. I wanted to be an American."

On September 12, 1978, three years after his escape from Saigon, Matt's dream came true. At a ceremony in Columbus, Ohio, with his family in attendance, the boy who was once Hoang Van Long, an orphan from Vietnam, officially became Matthew Ray Steiner, American citizen.

He had achieved his goal. At last he felt that he was a real American boy.

Matt's sixth-grade picture, taken as he is about to become an American citizen

RETURN TO VIETNAM

Matt remembers the photo that triggered his desire to explore his past.

He was in college, taking a history course that included a study of the Vietnam War—a subject he had always avoided, just as he had managed to avoid anything that touched on who he once was. He thought of himself only as Matthew Ray Steiner from West Liberty, Ohio.

But in his textbook was a picture of Amerasian children living on the streets of Saigon during the war. "I stared at it, filled with a sense of recognition," Matt recalls. "I remembered such children. I once looked like them. Had circumstances been slightly different, I could have *been* one of the children in the photo."

Suddenly he wanted to know everything about the war. He learned how devastating warfare had been on the country of his birth and that huge numbers of people had tried, and failed, to get out at the end when South Vietnam was collapsing.

Since the war, more than a million Vietnamese had left illegally by boat, determined to escape the harsh Communist government and the food shortages and poverty. Thousands had died on the open seas.

"For the first time, I understood how fortunate I had been not only to escape but to be adopted and to come to the United States," Matt says. "I wanted to return to Vietnam and learn more about the culture and the people. I was ready to explore my Vietnamese heritage."

The summer of 1995, when Matt was twenty-nine, he had that opportunity. Vietnam was ending its long isolation from western countries and opening its doors to visitors, even those from its former enemy, the United States. Matt learned he could tour Vietnam with John Williams, who had worked for Holt in Saigon and had since become president of Holt International. He decided to go.

~

As his plane flew over the Pacific Ocean toward Vietnam, Matt thought about the previous few years. In 1984 he had graduated as valedictorian of his high school, and in the fall of his senior year of college, he had decided to become a doctor and to practice medicine the way his father did, with compassion and charity for all. He had seen how his father took time with every patient, getting to know the person as well as the illness. He wanted to do the same.

He had written a letter to his father, sharing his decision to study medicine. He closed with "I appreciate all you've done for me in my life, Dad. I love you very much."

Then, the week before Christmas 1987, Matt received devastating news. A car had hit his father while he was jogging along a country road. Matt rushed to join his mother and brothers at his father's bedside.

"I knew he was going to die and that I could do nothing about it. It was like having a knife stuck in my stomach—so painful I couldn't stand it. I loved my dad so much! I was a six-year-old boy again, losing my beloved parent, and I was completely helpless," Matt says sadly.

"It took me a long time to work through my grief. Dad's death made me more determined than ever to be a doctor—to do it for him, as well as for me."

Worried about his mother, Matt took off the year after college to live with her and work at their local hospital. Then he completed his four years of medical school and moved to Indianapolis for his medical residency in emergency medicine.

At a New Year's Eve party in 1994, he met Laura Gamble, who was also studying to be a doctor. She had a lively intellect and beautiful dark hair and eyes. Matt was smitten.

Now he and Laura were planning to be married. Soon Matt would launch his medical career. When Matt decided to visit Vietnam, Laura couldn't go because she couldn't leave her medical studies, but Mary Steiner could, and she was eager to share her son's journey to his homeland.

Matt intended to keep his expectations low. It was still painful to think about his birth mother and Ba. Even if his grandmother was still alive, he didn't know where she lived. Nor did he want to try to locate other relatives. Not only did he have no way to do that, but he also felt no need. "The Steiners are my family," he says simply.

As his plane approached Saigon (though officially known as Ho Chi Minh City, many still call it Saigon), Matt was flooded with memories of the day twenty years before when he had left the country. "I remembered how excited I was to be on my way to America to my new family. But I also remembered the heat and the confusion, the fear of enemy attack, and my sadness at leaving Ba behind," he says. "Now I was looking out my window at the intense patchwork of lush greens below, and I could hardly believe that it seemed so peaceful."

Matt thought he would be an ordinary American tourist, but when he went through customs at Tan Son Nhut Airport, the official kept staring at him, examining his passport and identification papers over and over. Speaking a language Matt could no longer understand, the official forced him to step aside while others were checked through. Several other supervisors were summoned to look at Matt's documents. They eyed him suspiciously.

His passport revealed that he was from there, though he was now an American citizen.

"I don't know what they were thinking, but they made me feel very uneasy," Matt recalls. "Over an hour later, they handed back my passport and allowed me to leave. I kept reminding myself that Vietnam was a Communist country. Its relations with the United States were shaky. Maybe they were surprised that someone who had left would voluntarily come back."

When Matt, his mother, and John Williams were finally able to leave the airport and walk outside, Matt was startled by his instant sense of recognition. It all came back: the intense heat, the smells of the vast, sprawling city, the vegetation and trees, the singsong sound of the language, the architecture of the buildings, and the sights and sounds of the ever-present street markets.

"Everything was familiar. I had the sense that I was home," he says. "The heavy traffic, the noises, the smell of food cooking on the streets, the spicy *nuoc mam* fish sauce I love, the cyclos and motorbikes, and the river—I knew all of it. I think it had been lying dormant in me all those years."

He also began to recall simple words or phrases in Vietnamese. They came to his lips as needed, always surprising him. "I remembered words like *left* and *right*, and I knew the names of foods and how to say a few things. I was as surprised as everyone else when I would pop out with something."

When the three of them stopped in a small noodle shop for their first meal, Matt already knew what the food would taste like. While sightseeing on the streets, Matt knew that around the corner there would be a movie theater—the one where he saw *King Kong* all those years ago—and there it was. He remembered the park he had often visited. Soon he was watching for the alleys where he had played tag. He tried to locate the apartment where he and his grandmother had lived, but could not find it.

When Matt visited Saigon in 1995, he found a city that is a striking blend of old and new

*The midday sun can take a toll, and any spot in the shade is a good place for
a nap. Today, Saigon street life looks much as it always has, with street
markets and vendors supplying every need*

In the countryside, they stopped at several villages. Matt could not identify the village where he had lived for a year and where his mother had taken her own life. But once again, forgotten memories were reawakened when he saw small children running around barefoot, just as he had, and boys tending the giant lumbering water buffaloes.

"I wanted to be a buffalo boy," he told his mother. "That was my goal. Never in a million years would I have believed that one day I would live in America and become a doctor."

Back in Saigon, he ate one of the meat sandwiches sold by sidewalk vendors—the same kind his grandmother had bought him several times. Memories of Ba flooded over him, and he could barely finish it.

Later that same afternoon he visited the former Holt Center, where he had lived for almost two years, now empty and scheduled to be torn down to make way for a new building. In his memory, everything was huge. In reality, the walled playground and the rooms of the center were modest in size. He remembered the wall where children stood to have their pictures taken, and he saw the old cafeteria. The coverings over the rooftop classroom were still in place, and he vividly recalled his days on that roof, learning English and wondering if there would ever be a family who would want him.

During the ten-day trip, whenever he was around children, Matt's heart went out to them. "Holt was expanding its presence in Vietnam, and a highlight for me was visiting the three centers they've set up to feed hungry children and care for orphans," he says. "I was really pleased to learn that Holt is still helping orphans find adoptive homes, some of them in the United States."

At visits to several orphanages Holt helps sponsor, Matt and his mother distributed toys and medicine they had brought along. Matt assisted with medical evaluations of ill children and advised staff on up-to-date treatments. He played games with some of the children. Often he choked back

During his trip to Vietnam, Matt especially enjoyed time spent with children at orphanages

tears. "I saw myself in all of them. Like these children, I had once counted on the kindness and charity of others. I wished that I had more to give them."

John Williams had been back to Saigon several times since the war. He had managed to locate some of the former Holt staff members and took Matt to visit one of the teachers who had worked with Miss Anh. The teacher did not know what had happened to Miss Anh or where she now lived, but she remembered Matt and reminisced with him about the classroom on the rooftop.

"I can't describe how wonderful it felt to meet someone who had known me twenty years before," Matt says. "We talked about everything that happened at Holt, and laughed together about some of the silly things. I think she enjoyed it as much as I did."

Then the teacher began to talk about how difficult things had been since the war. She told Matt how the lives of ordinary Vietnamese had been filled with hardship. They never had enough food. Everyone was very poor. But their greatest fear was the harsh government that sought to punish anyone who had not supported North Vietnam during the war. People suffered terribly, she said. Many had been arrested and sent off to "re-education" camps. Many never returned, or only returned years later, bent and broken from their time in the camps. Amerasians like Matt were often singled out for special punishments. "It is better now," she said, "but be glad you were not here then."

She wanted to know how Matt had come to be at Holt. "I told her about my birth mother and about Ba," Matt says. "Then I shared how my birth mother had once tried to give me away to a wealthy couple who lived on a plantation. She didn't seem surprised. Instead, she just nodded and said, 'Your mother was seeking a better life for you.' "

Matt told her that Ba had taken him to the Holt Center and left him there, and how hard that was for him. "I missed her so much and I kept waiting for her to come and take me home with her," he said.

The teacher was quiet for a moment. "Your grandmother must have loved you very, very much to give you up," she said gently. "She could have kept you for her own, and what would have happened to you?"

Matt fought down the lump in his throat. "I always wished I could have stayed with her. I felt so alone without her."

"But she saw a chance for you to have a future," the teacher replied. She nodded approvingly at Mary Steiner, who sat nearby. "Your Ba's heart told her it would work out this way for you."

Matt felt something inside him shift. There had been a hole in his heart ever since his mother's death. When Ba left him at Holt, it grew larger. He had tried for twenty years to ignore it, realizing how fortunate he was in his new life and how much he loved the Steiner family. But the ache was still there.

Sitting with the teacher in her tiny Saigon apartment, Matt finally understood why Ba and his mother had made the choices they did. He felt at peace with his past.

When it was time to leave, he embraced the teacher for a long, long moment, trying to find the words to thank her for what she had given him.

~

Today, when Matt thinks of his grandmother, he realizes that, like so many people in Vietnam, the war had cost her dearly. She had lost her daughter and other family members. She had struggled daily to survive, working hard into her old age. There must have been many times when she was afraid, many times when she was in danger. And then she had to make the awful decision to give up her grandson.

"I know now that it was an act of courage and love on her part," Matt says. "My regret is that she never knew how well things worked out for me. I wish we could have stayed in touch after I left the country. I would have treasured that.

"I no longer feel that my birth mother abandoned me when she took her own life. As an adult and as a physician, I understand that she was probably severely depressed," he says. "I have seen patients who feel so overwhelmed with life that they no longer want to live. Perhaps today my mother could get treatment. But that didn't exist then. I'll never really be over her suicide, but I have accepted it. Rather than blame her, I appreciate everything she did for me."

Matt is a husband and father today and would like to take his children to Vietnam to visit. "I'd like them to feel pride in their Vietnamese roots. I'll tell them the story of my life and about my Vietnamese family. I'll tell them about my mother, and that once I had a grandmother just as wonderful as their grandma Mary, and because she loved me so much, she made a plan for me to be adopted so I could have a future.

"I want my children to know that war isn't just about guns and soldiers, that families get separated and many innocent people are killed. But even in the middle of war, sometimes good things happen. In this war, there were people trying to help kids like me. I'll tell them I was one of the lucky ones, because I was able to escape and I had a wonderful family waiting for me.

"I love my adopted country and I'm proud to be an American. But I will never forget that my American heart is half Vietnamese."

Matt and his wife, Laura, are the proud parents of Christian and Kate

AFTERWORD

POSTSCRIPT ON PEOPLE IN THE BOOK

Matt Steiner is an emergency room physician in Indiana. His wife, Laura, is also a practicing physician. They are the parents of Kate and Christian. When Matt and Laura married, Matt's brothers were his groomsmen.

Mary Steiner has remarried and is now Mary Psolla. She still lives in the family home in West Liberty, Ohio. Matt's brothers and their families are close by.

John Williams, former president and CEO of Holt International Children's Services in Eugene, Oregon, is now director of the Peace Corps in Thailand. He was a guest at Matt and Laura's wedding.

Glen Noteboom lives in Palm Springs, California. He recently retired from his job of doing adoption home studies for Holt and other agencies.

Bob Chamness is deceased.

Matt's teacher, **Miss Anh**, and Tai's mother, **Lan**, are real people whose names as well as identifying details have been changed, both to protect them and to respect their privacy.

OPERATION BABYLIFT

For many Americans, the rescue of the orphans airlifted from Saigon was the one bright spot in the otherwise bleak landscape of the Vietnam War. Like Matt, the children arriving in the United States, Canada, Australia,

An American crewman feeds one of the babies aboard an Operation Babylift flight

and throughout Europe via Operation Babylift were instant celebrities.

In three days' time, planes dispatched by the American government and by private agencies, such as Holt International and Friends For All Children, airlifted to safety approximately 2,300 orphaned children, almost all of whom had already been assigned to adoptive homes abroad. President Gerald Ford flew to San Francisco to greet the first Babylift plane and carry the first orphan onto American soil.

The airlift had no precedent in history. Americans and people of other nationalities had adopted European and Korean orphans after World War II and the Korean War, but their passage to their new homes had been arranged by the agencies sponsoring the adoptions.

INTERNATIONAL ADOPTION

When the American government got involved in Operation Babylift, some people questioned the idea of removing orphaned children from their homelands to grow up in countries where they would be minorities and possibly be subjected to discrimination.

But this risk had to be weighed against the prospect of leaving these children in a country lacking resources to care for them. Far more children died of malnutrition, injury, illness, and neglect than ever got into stable care and finally to adoptive homes abroad. International and Vietnamese humanitarian groups, including Catholic and other religious orders, tried to help the children. Their efforts were heroic, but never enough. In some remote orphanages, where malnutrition was rampant, it was not uncommon for every single child to die when there was an outbreak of measles, dysentery, or one of many other diseases prevalent in poor nations.

The relief agencies placing children for adoption focused on children with no known relatives. A few, like Holt International, also accepted some children—Matt among them—whose parent or guardian had relinquished the child to the agency.

Most agencies had only the children's best interests at heart. But many groups got involved in the crush and confusion of the fall of Saigon, and subsequent claims challenged that some Vietnamese children who were airlifted and then placed in adoptive homes were not actually orphans. This remains an area of controversy, even decades later.

Not all children who went to adoptive homes in other countries

adapted to their new lives as readily as did Matt. Because of the emotional
and physical stress most of them had experienced before they reached stable
homes, many have had long-term problems, ranging from ongoing physical problems to disabling emotional and learning problems. Some have
suffered from feelings of displacement and isolation. They wonder what
happened to their birth families, or they grieve for birth families they

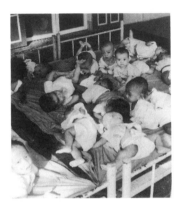 

*Life was difficult in orphanages during the war because few people were
available to take care of large numbers of children (top). But kids had
fun, too, like these youngsters learning to ride tricycles (bottom)*

remember. Some have not felt accepted by their new families or have suffered imaginary or real discrimination. Still, most recognize that international adoption gave them the opportunity for a new life.

THE AMERASIAN CHILDREN

A significant number of the children adopted from South Vietnam were Amerasian, fathered by U.S. servicemen. No one knows exactly how many Amerasian children were born during the Vietnam War. A conservative estimate is 40,000. Because the Vietnamese have always been sensitive to "outsiders," they can be biased against anyone of mixed race. Some Viet-

Glen Noteboom, an American social worker at the Holt Center, risked his life helping Holt children escape from Saigon in the closing days of the war

Peik Larsen, an Amerasian child at an orphanage near Danang, was reunited on a visit to Vietnam with the Sister who had helped care for him as a baby. Peik grew up in Cambridge, Massachusetts

namese referred to the Amerasian children as *bui doi*, meaning *the dust of life*. Because it could be very difficult for mothers to survive economically if they had mixed-race children, they sometimes chose to place their children with agencies that could provide a better life for them in adoptive homes overseas.

After the war, some Amerasian children, particularly those without families to protect them, did suffer discrimination. In 1987 the American government sponsored the Homecoming Act, giving permission for Amerasian children and their families to emigrate to America, and more than 22,000 Amerasians resettled here.

STATISTICS OF THE WAR

• Two to three million Vietnamese died during the Vietnam War (from 1954 to 1975), along with several hundred thousand soldiers and civilians in bordering Laos and Cambodia.

• At least a quarter million South Vietnamese were sentenced to "re-education" camps after the reunification of the country.

• During America's involvement in the war, of the 3.3 million Americans who served, 58,000 died and 2,000 were classified as missing in action. More than 300,000 Americans were wounded, many of them disabled for life. These statistics include medical personnel. About 10,000 American women served in the war. The majority were in the military and were nurses.

• The current population of the Socialist Republic of Vietnam is 81 million.

MULTIMEDIA RECOMMENDATIONS

FOR YOUNG READERS

Children of Vietnam, by Marybeth Lorbiecki (Minneapolis: Carolrhoda Books, 1997). A look at the lives of children in contemporary Vietnam, with simple explanations of its culture and history. Lovely color photos. *Sweet Dried Apples*, by Rosemary Breckler (Boston: Houghton Mifflin, 1996). A touching tale about two Vietnamese children whose village is bombed during the Vietnam War. *Vietnam*, by Karen O'Connor (Minneapolis: Carolrhoda Books, 1999). An engaging book about the land, the people, and their daily lives. *Water Buffalo Days*, by Huynh Quang Nhuong (New York: Harper Trophy, 1999). The author recounts in charming fashion his childhood growing up in a Vietnamese village, where his best friend was the family water buffalo.

FOR MIDDLE READERS

Cultures of the World: Vietnam, by Audrey Seah (New York: Marshall Cavendish, 1994). Excellent introduction to the people, their history, and culture. Three books by Bobbie Kalman: *Vietnam: The Land*; *Vietnam: The Culture*; *Vietnam: The People* (New York: Crabtree Publishing, 1996). The author uses simple text and excellent photos to introduce readers to Vietnam. *In Vietnam*, by Denis J. Hauptly (New York: Atheneum, 1985). Clear explanations of Vietnam's history, the conflict between North and South, and America's involvement. *The Story of the Saigon Airlift*, by Zachary Kent (Chicago: Children's Press, 1991). Photos and simple text explain the last month in Saigon before it fell to the North Vietnamese. *The Land I Lost*, by Huynh Quang Nhuong (New York: Harper Trophy, 1986). Fifteen tales by the author of *Water Buffalo Days* about his boyhood in South Vietnam. (The author is now a U.S. citizen.)

Two books, *The Vietnam Antiwar Movement in American History*, by Anita Louise McCormick (Berkeley Heights, N.J.: Enslow Publishers, 2000), and *The Vietnam War*, by Roger Barr (San Diego: Lucent Books, 1991), work well with *The Vietnam War: A History of U.S. Involvement*, by John M. Dunn (San Diego: Lucent Books, 2001) to provide an overview of America's war in Vietnam, offering clear explanations about the ground war, the politics, and the protests back home in America.

FOR MATURE READERS

Dispatches, by Michael Herr (New York: Avon Books, 1978). A classic journal of war. *In Country*, by Bobbie Ann Mason (New York: HarperCollins, 1986). A coming-of-age novel about a teenage girl whose father was killed in Vietnam and whose uncle is a Vietnam vet. *Tears Before the Rain: An Oral History of the Fall of South Vietnam*, by Larry Engelmann (New York: Da-Capo Press, 1997). Voices of Vietnamese and Americans who were there. *The Things They Carried*, by Tim O'Brien (Broadway Books, 1998). A collection of twenty-two interrelated short pieces that together form a whole. All relate to the Vietnam War. Some are fiction; some are based on the author's experiences as an American GI in that war. *The Unwanted: A Memoir of Childhood*, by Kien Nguyen (Boston: Little, Brown, 2001). A memoir by an Amerasian who now lives in the U.S. about the devastating years following reunification in Vietnam, and the suffering he and his family endured. *Vietnam: A History*, by Stanley Karnow (New York: Viking Press, 1983). A comprehensive history of the war, with special emphasis on America's role. *Vietnam, Now: A Reporter Returns*, by David Lamb (New York: PublicAffairs, 2002) A fascinating journey through modern Vietnam, told by a reporter who covered the war, then went back to live there in 1997 and discovered a whole new country. *When Heaven and Earth Changed Places* (New York: Doubleday, 1989) and *Child of War, Woman of Peace* (New York: Bantam Doubleday Dell, 1993), both by Le Ly Hayslip. The author was a village child during the war and grew up to marry an American GI and live in the U.S.

RECOMMENDED WEB SITE

http://www.vvmf.org. Sponsored by the Vietnam Veterans Memorial Fund. Click on "Teach Vietnam" to explore a remarkable Web site that includes history, reflection, photos, and links with other quality, updated Web sites Very well done and useful for students and educators.

A Web site search for "Vietnam War" and "Operation Babylift" will bring up a variety of sites and information. Keep in mind that groups often have a specific agenda, and it's possible that not all the information given will be reliable.

VIDEOS

Vietnam: A Television History. This Emmy-winning seven-volume series presents a detailed study of the war and its aftermath. Contains graphic material. Written by Andrew Pearson, produced by WGBH Educational Foundation, Boston. *Precious Cargo*. Produced for PBS, this documentary follows eight adoptees from Vietnam on their journey back to their homeland in search of their past.

MOVIES

Hollywood has its own versions of the Vietnam War. With the exception of *Indochine*, which views the coming war from the French perspective (and is in French with English subtitles), all of the notable movies listed here relate stories of American soldiers before, during, and/or after the war.

About the War

Apocalypse Now, Born on the Fourth of July, Coming Home, The Deer Hunter, Full Metal Jacket, Hair (based on the musical of the same name), *Hamburger Hill, In Country, Indochine, Platoon, We Were Soldiers*. Because of graphic violence, parental discretion is urged.

About Vietnam

Cyclo, The Scent of Green Papaya, Three Seasons, The Vertical Rays of the Sun. These four fine movies have all been produced by Vietnamese directors using Vietnamese actors. They realistically portray Vietnamese culture.

SOURCES

Like many writers whose subject matter has been Vietnam, I found I could not do it justice until I actually visited that tiny country, experiencing for myself the landscape, the culture, the warmth of the people, and the ghosts of war. I believe that firsthand experience has brought accuracy of detail to many passages in this book.

In addition to the invaluable help of eyewitness accounts from Matt Steiner and from men and women I've cited elsewhere who were in Saigon and participated in Operation Babylift, I found the following texts helpful: *The Fall of Saigon*, by David Butler (New York: Simon and Schuster, 1985); *Orphans of War*, by Rosemary Taylor (London: William Collins Sons & Co., 1988); and *Tears Before the Rain: An Oral History of the Fall of South Vietnam*, by Larry Engelmann (New York: DaCapo Press, 1997).

I have long been interested in the story of the orphaned children of South Vietnam and in Operation Babylift, and I began collecting materials and interviewing eyewitnesses shortly after the end of the war. In graduate school, I explored American magazine coverage of the Babylift in my thesis, and I repeatedly turned to that thesis for assistance while writing this book. Thus, it, too, was an important source: "Operation Babylift and the Adoption of Vietnamese Orphans: The Coverage Given By Four American Magazines, 1975–1976," by Andrea Warren (M.S. thesis, University of Kansas, 1983). I also referred to a first-person narrative article I wrote for the May

1999 issue of the journal *The World & I* titled "The Angels of Vietnam," in which I related the story of my daughter's return to Vietnam in search of her own past.

Other sources I consulted include: *Cultures of the World: Vietnam*, by Audrey Seah (New York: Marshall Cavendish, 1994); *Encyclopedia of the Vietnam War*, edited by Stanley I. Kutler (New York: Charles Scribner's Sons, 1996); *Fire in the Lake: The Vietnamese and the Americans in Vietnam*, by Frances FitzGerald (New York: Back Bay Books, 2002); *For Children Cannot Wait*, by Susan Carol McDonald, S.L. (Columbus, Ohio: Brown Graphic Press, 1980); *A Home for Every Child*, by John Aeby (Eugene, Oregon: Holt International Children's Services, 1986); *The Home Front: Americans Protest the War*, by Stuart A. Kallen (San Diego: Lucent Books, 2001); *Vietnam: A History*, by Stanley Karnow (New York: Viking Press, 1983); "Vietnam Now," by Stanley Karnow, *Smithsonian*, January 1996, pp. 34–42; and *The Vietnam War Almanac*, edited by John S. Bowman (New York: World Almanac Publications, 1985).

ACKNOWLEDGMENTS

I am grateful to many individuals for their assistance with this project. I could not have written it without the full cooperation of Matt Steiner, who, in spite of an incredibly busy schedule as a husband, father, and physician, cheerfully worked with me endless hours so we could get the story right. I am also grateful to Matt's mother, Mary Steiner Psolla, who contributed her memories and a careful record of what happened when; John Williams and Glen Noteboom, formerly of Holt's Saigon Center, who were part of Operation Babylift; Susan McDonald, a Sister of Loretto, who worked with the orphaned children of South Vietnam and also participated in the Babylift; Mary Nelle Gage, a Sister of Loretto, and Peggy Hammond, volunteers in South Vietnam, for assistance with memories and photos; Barbara Bartocci and Deborah Shouse, who stuck it out with me, week to week; Susie Nightingale, Sandra Lamb, John Aeby, and Latha Meyer for technical help; my agent, Regina Ryan, who was encouraging from start to finish; and my editor at Farrar, Straus and Giroux, Melanie Kroupa, who shared my vision for this book. Finally, I must mention in loving gratitude my husband, Jay Wiedenkeller, who lives the ups and downs with me, and never complains.

PHOTO CREDITS

INDEX